I NEVER WANTED TO BE A TEACHER

MY JOURNEY TO INSPIRING CHANGE AND COMBATING THE TEEN SUBSTANCE ABUSE AND MENTAL HEALTH CRISES

PAUL VECCHIONE

Tarafied
PUBLISHING CO.

Paperback ISBN: 979-8-9986159-0-0

Hardcover ISBN: 979-8-9986159-1-7

Cover design by Paul Vecchione

Edited by Tara Hayes

Interior layout by Kevin R Coleman

10 9 8 7 6 5 4 3 2 1

For permissions, inquiries, or bulk orders, contact: p.vecchione@longislandprep.org

Published with the Assistance of Tarafied Publishing LLC

https://www.tarafiedpublishing.com/

"Two roads diverged in a wood, and I—

I took the one less traveled by,

And that has made all the difference."

— ROBERT FROST

CONTENTS

PART IV

EFFECTIVE SOLUTIONS

ACKNOWLEDGMENTS

To my wife, **Melanie**—The center of my universe, my best friend, and life partner. Thank you for your unwavering encouragement, support, and inspiration. You are the closest embodiment of unconditional love that exists on this earth.

To **Nicholas, Matthew, and Dominic**—For showing me the world through a father's eyes and providing me with the motivation to make even the smallest difference in your lives and the lives of others.

To **Robert, Rosalie, Bobby, Michael, and Michelle**—For shaping me into the person I am today. Your love, wisdom, life lessons, loyalty, and support over the years have been my foundation.

To **John, Joanna, Christina, and Janine**—For making me part of your family since the beginning. Your love and support for Melanie and me, and our boys, has been a consistent staple in our lives always.

To **Tim Sini**—The closest person I have to another brother. Thank you for your devotion to our friendship, for being my reflection, for challenging me to grow, and for your steadfast support over the years.

To **Mr. Murphy, Mr. Zocchia, and Mr. Pitagno**—For inspiring me to become an educator. You taught me so much about the power of teaching and inspiring young people to try their best, be their best, and enjoy learning.

To **My Lunch Crew, The Power and The K's**—if you know, you know. I am forever grateful for your friendship.

To **Dr. Frank Robert Maurio**—For helping me uncover the untapped potential within me and guiding me through its discovery. Your belief in me made all the difference.

To **the parents, families, and friends who have lost loved ones to the struggles of mental health and addiction,** your pain is immeasurable. We honor you for your strength, your resilience, and your unwavering dedication to illuminating the legacy of those you have lost. May their stories never be forgotten, and may their struggles inspire the change we so desperately need.

You are not alone.

To my students—past, present, and future—You have been my greatest teachers. Your stories, struggles, and triumphs have shaped me in ways I never could have imagined. You've taught me resilience, patience, and the power of human connection. You've challenged me, inspired me, and given me purpose.

This book is for you.

May you always believe in your worth, embrace your potential, and never stop fighting for the life you deserve.

LETTER TO PARENTS

Dear Parents,

First, let me say thank you. Thank you for picking up this book, for caring deeply about the challenges our children face, and for believing in the collective effort it takes to safeguard their future. As a parent myself, I know that raising children in today's world is no small task. It's a journey filled with joy and pride, but also with worry, uncertainty, and the weight of knowing that the choices we make today will shape the lives of the next generation.

This book is my way of inviting you on a journey—a journey through my experiences, struggles, and triumphs, and most importantly, a journey toward creating a brighter future for our kids. Over the years, I've worn many hats: parent, teacher, advocate, and someone who has faced my battles with anxiety, self-doubt, and who understands the lure of addiction. Each of these roles has taught me invaluable lessons about humility, empathy, and the power of resilience.

As a teacher, I spent two decades immersed in the lives of teenagers. I witnessed firsthand the growing mental health crisis, the devastating impact of substance abuse, and the crushing pressures that weigh on our children every day. I saw their struggles and triumphs, and I learned that addressing these issues requires more than classroom lessons—it requires *a holistic approach that involves families, schools, and communities working together.*

Through my battles, I learned what it means to ask for help, to confront challenges head-on, and to come out stronger on the other side. These experiences ignited my passion to do more—to create programs and initiatives that not only educate but empower young people to face life's challenges with confidence and resilience. That passion is what led to the creation of Long Island PREP, an organization dedicated to addressing the root causes of substance abuse and mental health struggles and equipping kids with the tools they need to thrive.

This book will take you through the moments that shaped me, from growing up in a loving community to finding my way as an educator and advocate. It will shine a light on the failures of the past to address the critical issues our children face and show how life lessons have inspired a new approach—one that focuses on prevention, compassion, and collaboration. You'll see how every experience I've had, from the challenges of my own life to the lessons learned in the classroom, has come together to fuel this mission.

Most importantly, this book is about hope. It's about the belief that we can do better for our children, that we can create a world where they feel supported, empowered, and understood. It's about working together— parents, educators, and communities—to build a foundation that safeguards their future. Thank you for placing your faith in me to take this fight forward. Thank you for your commitment to the well-being of our children and fostering the belief that together, not only can we make a difference, we can BE the difference.

I'm honored to have you join me on this journey and grateful for the opportunity to share it with you.

With gratitude,

Paul Vecchione M.A., B.A., B.S.

LETTER TO MY CHILDREN

To Nicholas and Matthew,

You hold all of the hope I have for the future. You are living in tumultuous times, and as you grow, so do the challenges. Embrace them and remember that nothing worthwhile is easy. Always lean on who you are, not who others want you to be. Every single thing we do is for you, and let the lessons we passed guide you along the way.

To Dominic,

You are the embodiment of resilience, the living proof that struggles can shape, but never define us. In you, I see the strength forged from my challenges, the hope that emerged from moments of doubt, and the unwavering purpose that has guided me forward. You are my greatest reminder that perseverance leads to something far greater than success—it leads to life.

With all my love,
Dad

FOREWORD

BY DWIGHT "DOC" GOODEN, 3X WORLD SERIES CHAMPION

Life doesn't always go the way we plan. I know that better than most. When I was a kid growing up in Tampa, baseball was my everything. It gave me a purpose, a dream, and eventually, a career that took me to the top of the world. Even when you think you have it all—talent, money, fame—you can still find yourself lost.

Addiction doesn't care who you are. It doesn't care about your past, your achievements, or the people who love you. It sneaks up on you, grabs hold, and doesn't let go without a fight. I've had my battles and I've made my share of mistakes. But I also know that redemption is possible. I know that no matter how deep you fall, there's always a way back. That's what this book is about.

But overcoming addiction isn't just about willpower. It's about mental health. For too long, people—especially athletes, men, and those in the public eye—have been afraid to talk about what's really going on inside. We're taught to be strong, push through pain, to never show weakness. But staying silent only makes things worse. I've learned that true strength comes from being honest about your struggles, seeking help, and surrounding yourself with people who support you.

When approached to write the foreword for this book, I had to consider the purpose of my own experiences and the purpose of what this book is really meant to achieve. Because the truth is, guiding youth down the path to success goes beyond just words. It involves a global effort by everyone in a child's life. Parents and family, educators, coaches, and the community. That is what this book is all about, and that is what Paul Vecchione hopes to accomplish with his work.

This isn't just a story of struggle—it's a guide for resilience. It's a reminder that overcoming life's obstacles isn't just about personal survival but about making sure the next generation learns from our mistakes. If my experiences can help even one person avoid the same pitfalls, then they were not in vain.

To the young people reading this, know that the choices you make today will shape your tomorrow. Surround yourself with people who truly care about you, stay focused on your goals, and never be afraid to ask for help. No one gets through this life alone.

To those in the middle of their battles, I want you to know that it's never too late. There's always hope, always another chance, always a path forward if you're willing to take it.

Your mind is just as important as your body. Take care of it. Talk about what you're going through. There's no shame in it—only strength.

This book is a testament to that belief. I hope it helps you find the courage to keep going.

Dwight "Doc" Gooden

INTRODUCTION

I founded Long Island PREP with one clear purpose—helping kids, their parents, and their teachers navigate life's challenges and build resilience for the future. The name might not roll off the tongue, but its mission has always been solid: to equip the next generation with the tools they need to grow into strong, capable adults.

LONG ISLAND
P.R.E.P
Prevention and Resilience Enrichment Program

P.O. Box 201
Babylon, NY 11702
www.longislandprep.org

Substance Abuse Prevention
Mental Wellness Awareness
Intervention Services

Paul Vecchione
Founder, CEO

When I launched Long Island PREP in 2017, I knew I had to commit fully. Too many times in my life, I had ideas I never followed through on—whether because the timing wasn't right or unexpected challenges got in the way. But this was different. If I were going to invest my time, energy, and resources into something meaningful, I was determined to see it through.

Everything that you will read in this story connects back to the foundation of Long Island PREP—a vision shaped by my real experiences, the lessons I've learned, and my unwavering belief that we can help the next generation be stronger and more prepared than ever before.

Paul Vecchione

PART I

MY ROOTS

1

HUMILIATION

"I t was the best of times…"

Well, at least for me, it was. It beats starting with, "For as far back as I can remember, I always wanted to be a gangster," right? But seriously, how cliché to begin what might be the only book I'll ever write with the famously overused line from Dickens. Still, when I reflect on the last 45 years of my life, I can't help but feel like I've lived smack dab in the middle of a storybook beginning.

Born to two salt-of-the-earth parents of Italian descent, I grew up in a suburban enclave with hallmarks of the American Dream. My life, while sparing you the most intimate details, came with every perk you could imagine for a white male in post-WWII-era America—a legacy of hope, opportunity, and upward mobility handed down from parents and grandparents who worked hard to ensure it.

We had a big family rooted in deep values. My father, a hardworking business owner, built his exterminating business from the ground up. My mother, the cornerstone of our home, stayed at home to raise me, my two brothers, and my sister. Our upper-middle-class neighborhood was safe, wholesome, and close-knit, with great schools, great teachers, and a real sense of community.

We fished, boated, surfed, biked, paint balled, skateboarded, played kick the can and manhunt on warm summer evenings and celebrated birthdays and graduations with what seemed like endless streams of neighbors, friends and family and we played outside until the street lights came on, we had a bike path that cut through the fields of cattails and spartina plants and a marina to cast our lines out for snappers in the late summer. Landscapers in the neighborhood kept the smell of freshly cut grass in the air from daylight savings time to Halloween.

Some of the nicest beaches in America were only a 3-mile drive on the Robert Moses Causeway, which was just yards from the sprawling, five-bedroom colonial I grew up in. We were raised by the company we kept and the values they shared. Community, church, Little League baseball, street hockey, and spaghetti dinners at our elementary school were all staples in our lives growing up. I never actually asked, but I don't think my parents ever locked our doors at night.

One of my earliest childhood memories is of my dad vacuuming the pool in our backyard, which was not a luxurious in-ground oasis but a modest above-ground circle of water that was always too cold to swim in because it stood in the corner of our yard and was shaded by a neighbor's Japanese maple tree that blocked the warming rays of the midday sun.

My father worked six days a week but was always home for family dinners, a non-negotiable tradition. He built his business through relentless effort, and while his work was demanding, it came with rewards. We ate at nice restaurants, went on vacations three or four times a year, and always had the toys, gadgets, and perks that came from being the children of someone who worked tirelessly to provide for us.

"You have what you have because your father works hard and saves," my mom would remind us. Little did I know those words were among the greatest life lessons I'd ever receive.

My mother was there when we woke up in the morning until we went to sleep at night, always filling the house with everything we needed, including the best home-cooked meals you could ever imagine.

My parents didn't have to demand much because their expectations were clear: accountability, family first, work hard, get good grades, respect your elders, honor your heritage, and appreciate the life they'd built for us—a life that was not from generational wealth but of sacrifice, discipline, and values.

Looking back, I can say without hesitation that my life wasn't difficult. I grew up in a loving, supportive home filled with opportunity, morals, and values that shaped me into who I am today. And while hindsight certainly makes everything clearer, even at the time, I knew I was fortunate.

I could go on forever about how amazing it was to grow up the way I did, surrounded by the people and experiences that shaped me. It all fits perfectly into the theme of this story—a story that begins with the truth I never saw coming:

I never wanted to be a teacher.

Humiliation

As awesome as my childhood was, it wasn't always sunshine and butterflies. Life has a way of sneaking in moments that sting—some that fade over time and others that leave lasting scars. One of the most vivid and painful memories I have is a middle school nightmare that still makes me cringe. Everyone has their stories, but this one left a mark I'll never forget.

It all started with a rumor. At first, it was just whispers in the hallway. Then it escalated. I still remember walking up the small footbridge that connected the backstreets of our community to the high school parking lot. The bridge, a common fixture of our neighborhood, was usually just a nondescript shortcut. But on this autumn morning, it became the stage for one of the most humiliating moments of my life.

Spray-painted in bold, dark green letters on the light grey cement was my name, followed by an accusation, a pretty serious one that, for a young teenager, was tough to bear. On the walls of the bridge was so much more than graffiti; it was a public declaration of a vicious, fabricated rumor about something teenage boys might do in private moments—I'll let you read between the lines. I had been warned it was there by two classmates who called me at home before the school day began. I thought I was prepared to face it, but nothing could have prepared me for the pit in my stomach or the lump in my throat when I saw it in person.

In 1994, during the fragile, awkward years of early adolescence, something like this exceeded the boundaries of a mere joke—it was a character assassination. It was a public branding, designed to humiliate and ostracize. The comments, the whispers, the snickers—they all came in waves and didn't stop. Even my closest friends couldn't resist the occasional jab.

For two long years, that rumor followed me everywhere. It tarnished my social life and took a hit to my self-confidence. The situation hit its lowest point when I mustered the courage to ask a girl I liked on a date. She said yes, only to change her mind because a friend had convinced her to rescind, compliments of the rumor started about me years earlier.

To set the record straight: the claim was completely untrue. Just an out-of-nowhere declaration of war on my character, unprovoked and pure vitriol.

Years later, I ran into the person responsible for the rumor. He admitted that he had made it all up. He even apologized. His words might have been sincere, but by then, they didn't matter. The damage had already been done, and the scars remained.

What made it all so much harder was the isolation. I didn't feel like I could talk to anyone—not my parents, not my teachers, not even my closest friends. At 14 years old, I didn't have the emotional tools to navigate such an ugly time in my life. I kept it all inside, carrying the weight of the embarrassment alone.

Despite coming from a loving, supportive home and a strong community, the trials of adolescence still found their way to me. No matter how solid the foundation, growing up is never without its struggles. That chapter of my life, though painful, taught me so much about resilience and perseverance, and about the invisible battles so many people face.

Oddly enough, it fits like a glove with the theme of this story: I never wanted to be a teacher. But looking back, it's clear that those experiences—especially the difficult ones—shaped my perspective in ways that would later guide me in helping others, proof that even the darkest moments can eventually lead to the light.

2

THE BLIZZARD OF '96

By the middle of 10th grade, the sting of being the target of the nastiest rumor in the teenage world had finally faded. The attributes that truly defined who I was—friendly, smart, popular, and fun to be around—began to shine through again. Those qualities carried me through the remaining years of high school, where I found my stride. I had a great group of friends, good grades, a girlfriend, and, perhaps most importantly, a clearer vision of who I wanted to be, where I wanted to go, and how I might get there.

I've always been curious about everything—a kind of sponge for knowledge about subjects that caught my interest. History, writing, the Spanish language, marine science, and earth science—they all fascinated me. But there was one subject that stood above the rest: meteorology. Since I was a young boy, I wanted to study the weather. Imagine that! While my peers dreamed of careers as doctors, lawyers, or athletes, I was hoping to be summoned to the middle of a flood or hurricane to report on the impact.

And why? Because you can't discount the impact that weather can have on the world on a given day. There are undoubtedly infinite times when weather played a significant role in changing history. Good or bad. D-Day in 1944 was delayed due to the weather. In 1963, the bubble top of President Kennedy's limousine in Dallas was ordered off once the rain stopped that morning. In 1985, the Challenger disaster occurred after a cold front brought sub-freezing temperatures to Florida the night before launch. In 2001, there was severe weather up and down the eastern seaboard just hours before the doomed flights of September 11th took to the air. In any of these events, just a tweak in the weather conditions before, during, or after they took place would have changed the course of history.

Weather always fascinated me, and still does.

Growing up, I experienced hurricanes, floods, and blizzards. Each one piqued my interest in the weather even more.

The winter of 1996 was pivotal for me. It was one of the snowiest winters on record for Long Island, with storm after storm stretching well into April. But it wasn't just any winter. This was the winter of *the big one.*

Local news stations were buzzing about the storm for days. In the week leading up to it, "the models" started to align, and when they do that far in advance, it's usually a sign that something massive is on the way. Headlines like "18-24 inches with locally higher amounts" and "Near-blizzard conditions expected" flashed across The Weather Channel screen. For a 16-year-old interested in the weather, it really had my attention.

At the time, I was working part-time as a barback at Schooners, a local restaurant in town, but I was psyched for the pending storm. The Long Island region hadn't seen a storm like this in years; the winters of the '80s and early '90s were relatively mild. The excitement was everywhere—on the news, in school hallways, even at work. People were prepping for closures, stocking up on supplies, and talking about sledding plans at Captree Hill. There was a buzz around town, which piqued my interest even more.

And then, on Sunday, January 7, 1996, it hit.

The snow began falling late in the afternoon while I was at work, and it didn't stop for three days. I remember looking out the restaurant's windows as the snow came down harder and harder, blanketing the world in white. By the time the storm finally tapered off, schools were closed for four days, and the streets were nearly impassable. The dig-out that followed was monumental, and for me, it solidified my fascination with meteorology.

Experiencing the impact of a major snowstorm was really cool, and for me, it was the turning point. The Blizzard of '96 wasn't just a weather event; it was the moment I was convinced that meteorology was something I wanted to pursue.

After that, my mind was made up: I was going to be a meteorologist.

Because, after all, I never wanted to be a teacher.

3

DISILLUSIONMENT

Yeah, it didn't work out.

Looking back, it's easy to understand why I was drawn to the weather. I've always found it fascinating—the power, unpredictability, and universal impact of it. I wanted to be the person on TV warning about approaching storms, tracking the spin of an Atlantic cyclone, or reporting live from the center of it all. Weather is dynamic and humbling, and it captured my interest from an early age.

But as much as I loved it, my dream of becoming a meteorologist wasn't built to last. The reality of what it takes to predict the weather and make it in the field turned out to be much more complex than I imagined. Meteorology is an inexact science that involves predicting how the atmosphere will behave, now and in the future —it's an intricate dance of physics, chemistry, and intense mathematics. Local forecasts might look simple when they flash across your TV screen, but behind the scenes, meteorology is complicated and layered with many, many variables. And becoming an on-air meteorologist? That's a whole other mountain to climb. It's a career that starts in small, obscure markets, where you grind it out ,hoping to one day make it to a competitive big-city newsroom. Even then, success is far from guaranteed.

So, when it came time to choose a college during my senior year of high school, I decided that all but sealed the fate of my meteorology dreams. Instead of attending one of the atmospheric science programs I'd been accepted to—schools that could have set me on the right track—I chose Southampton College of Long Island University, a local college that was far enough to give me the experience of going away but close enough to home that I didn't have to leave the life I loved too far behind.

Looking back, I know it was the wrong choice for my dream, but at the time, I didn't have the foresight to understand how critical school choice was for a career in meteorology—or in any field. And honestly, I was more focused on the experience of college itself than on what I would do afterward. I studied weather, interned at a top national laboratory's weather station, and dived into broadcast journalism, landing internships at radio and TV stations, News 12 Long Island, WLIU, WEHM, and WBEA. But in the end, despite having the full college experience, with great friends and real-world education, I had the passion, but I lacked the foundation and the direction to make it happen.

I don't blame my parents. They supported me in every way they could, and as the first in my family to go to college, we were all navigating uncharted territory. Still, I sometimes wonder what might have been if we'd known more about the college process and how to choose a school that aligned with my dream. I guess when it was time to decide on a college, I figured I could always transfer if it didn't work out. But I had adjusted to and enjoyed my college experience so much that it didn't happen. It's a reminder that even with the best support system, making decisions about something as monumental as your future can be incredibly difficult.

I decided to stay at Southampton College because it had checked many boxes for deciding on a college. I was close to home, but I was also away at school. It had an intimate campus with small class sizes, it also had a great internship program that I was able to take advantage of right away. But let's face it, the college experience, especially those first few months as a freshman, is about liberation, living on your own, and your social life with the friends you meet, who experience the same thing as you.

I made many friends right from the start. There were students from all over the country, Maine, Connecticut, Georgia, Ohio, Wisconsin, Texas, and California, to name a few. Part of what makes me who I am is my intense curiosity. I always want to know more, learn more, ask more, and experience more. So socializing with people from all over the United States, as well as the world, had me caught up in the day-to-day college life of doing just that. One particular experience stands out the most to me.

Remembering where I came from, an upper-middle-class, mostly white community, had given me the very best upbringing imaginable, but it also gave me disillusionment about how the real world exists. Making friends in college was not only a blessing but a real eye-opener for me, and it would become the greatest life lesson I ever learned—observing the world around me as I see it and thinking for myself, not how others want me to think, or the prejudices they wanted me to have.

By the middle of my second semester, I had become friendly with a group of kids from New York City. Not Park Avenue, New York City, mind you. The South Bronx, Queens, and Brooklyn, New York City. People of African American, Hispanic, and other cultures and backgrounds that did not mirror mine at all.

They were real street kids, but I loved hanging around with them. They were loyal, fun, funny, always doing cool things, and always stuck together.

I learned more about the world in those first few months hanging out with those guys than at any other time in my life. I learned about the hardships some kids my age experienced. I learned about poverty, broken homes, single parents, growing up in bad neighborhoods on the streets, and the value of working hard just to have a meal. Many of these guys were on educational opportunities supported by government programs. So their education and room and board were paid for, but not their meal plans. So if they didn't work, they didn't eat.

Thanks to my parents' funding, I was lucky enough to always have cash in my ATM account. But it wasn't exuberant, and if I was going to take full advantage of college life, I would also have to work.

And because the work sucked, there were always jobs available in the student cafeteria. Marriott Food Services was the contracted vendor, and Gary was the supervisor, a serious all-business type of guy with no personality. The only thing Gary cared about was staffing the kitchen, scheduling, and staying under his budget. He was the quintessential boss, and, not mincing any words here, he was an asshole.

So, when I applied for a job with the food services, I landed in the cafeteria washing dishes for $5/hour. Not ideal, but sometimes the worst experiences bring the best outcomes.

Enter, Rafael Diaz, a 6'3", physically imposing kid from the South Bronx.

"Ralphie" as he was known was a rough and tumble street kid who everyone knew. He was loud and persistent. When Ralphie was in the room, everyone knew it, because everyone heard him. I had seen (and heard) Ralphie around campus all of the time and being the somewhat shy kid from the south shore of Long Island, I was intimidated by him at first.

My first day on the job, sure enough, Ralphie ended up on the other side of the dishwashing window handing me dirty dishes to wash. *Gulp.*

It all started innocently enough. Silence at first, dirty dish-rinse, stack, and repeat. The first hour Ralphie and I looked at each other like *okay, this sucks, we're both stuck there but who's going to speak first?* He didn't know me as much as I didn't know him, so we just did our duties, engaging in small talk. Nothing exciting.

Then, while passing me a dirty dish, Ralphie dropped it. *CRASH!*

The porcelain plate exploded in a thousand pieces and someone else's half eaten dinner went everywhere, including all over me and all over Ralphie. I remember looking up and seeing mashed potatoes in his goatee, the same mashed potatoes that were in my hair and eyebrows. The cafeteria went silent.

Remember that as you are finding your way in a new environment, everything around you is an audience to your stage. And all eyes in that cafeteria were on us after the cacophony of broken porcelain and the commotion it caused and the attention it drew.

What should I do? I remember thinking.

I could have summoned the sometimes pugnacious side of my personality and started yelling, which would have certainly brought an already awkward situation to a different level. And I was dealing with someone I didn't know at all. Someone bigger, heavier, and most certainly tougher than me.

No, not a good idea.

Truth be told, Ralphie could beat the shit out of me in about three seconds. So, I thought the better of it.

Yeah, no. "Thinking the better of it" meant keeping the pugnaciousness subdued, but not the antagonistic. It was a golden opportunity to take advantage of the situation and maybe score a point or two with the people in the packed cafeteria, watching our every move.

So as I leaned down to begin picking up the shattered plate and food on the floor, I decided to scrape some mashed potatoes off of my Marriott Food Services shirt and fling them at Ralphie. As they flew dead on toward him it was the *Christmas Story* moment when a different Ralphie was helping his father change a tire and sent the bolts flying.

Ohhhh Fuuccckk..

Praying they wouldn't, the mashed potatoes made it there.

Bam! Direct hit, right between his eyes!

Gulp.

I was dead, I was sure of it. He was going to hop through that dish-washing window and beat me senseless!

To my utter relief and bewilderment, that's not what happened at all. Instead, Ralphie burst into laughter.

He had this sneaky but infectious laugh that not only instantly diffused a tense situation but also invited others to partake. So I did. The sight of mashed potatoes dripping off of his face and him cracking up about it immediately had me in stitches.

I couldn't help myself, and the two of us stood there and laughed for what seemed like an eternity. But Ralphie, who was kind hearted but antagonistic in his own right, was also no push over. He wasn't going to allow this to happen without retaliation.

He shoved his baseball mitt-sized hand into a pile of food from a plate nearby and fired it at me with such ferocity that when it hit me, I was stunned. You guessed it, right between the eyes!

What followed was mayhem. Between the endless supply of ammo from the dirty plates within our reach and the long dishwasher hose that fired hot water with pressure and force, the two of us proceeded to have the food and water fight of the century in the middle of the student cafeteria. With everyone watching. Suddenly, their opinion of the situation and how we had reacted didn't matter. We were in full combat mode, and neither one of us would let up.

We were soaked to the bone, covered with half-eaten food, but we just kept going. I don't know how long it lasted. But it was epic, and we were gasping for air, laughing so hard throughout.

Eventually, Gary broke it up, escorting us both out of the student cafeteria and terminating our time with Marriott Food Services.

"You'll never work for us again".

Oh well, I thought.

Of all the emotions (and food) that filled the air that day, the most impactful one for me was relief.

I was happy Ralphie didn't just take that first shot of mashed potatoes to the face with anger and violence, because it was probably justified but it would not have ended well for me.

Instead, a lot of walls for me came down that day. Ralphie was big and strong and tough and aggressive and in your face.

But he was just as light-hearted and fun and gentle as I was. And that day, a friendship was born that is still intact today. They say college is not about what you learn in the classroom, but what you learn outside of the classroom and the people you meet. People who will become lifelong friends, and I can say from experience that there is simply no truer statement in the world.

I would go on to meet many more great people at Southampton and settle into my studies, but my initial dream didn't come true. I learned so much about atmospheric science, but never put it into action. I didn't realize at the time that this experience was setting the stage for something entirely different—a path I never wanted to take but one that would ultimately define my life.

The twists and turns that followed, the setbacks and new opportunities, would eventually lead me to a place I'd never imagined: the path to becoming a teacher. The dream I left behind wasn't the end of my story. It was the beginning of one I never saw coming.

4

I'M A GODDAMN EXTERMINATOR

As I've mentioned, I've always loved learning and have a knack for excelling in my studies. College was no exception—it was fun, fulfilling, and fluid. I graduated from Long Island University in 2002, *Magna Cum Laude*, with a degree in journalism. I was the first student to intern at the university's brand-new radio station and was a columnist for the school newspaper. I met great friends and had the experience of a lifetime while at college, and I don't regret a minute of the time I spent there, the people I met, the professors who helped guide me, and the foundation it helped me build for future success. But despite all of this, at 22 years old, I wasn't quite ready to leap into the professional workforce.

So, like many recent college grads who aren't ready for the 9-to-5 grind, I went back to school. With my experience in radio and newspaper journalism, I decided to pursue a master's degree in journalism and electronic media at the New York Institute of Technology. Without hesitation, I flew through the program with ease, earning *Magna Cum Laude* honors again in just 16 months. With my infinite interest in everything academic, being a student suited me. It also put off the inevitable progression of leaving my youth in the rearview for a full-time career, something I don't think I was ready for.

But by the winter of 2003, it became clear that with college behind me, I would have to start making that transition. I created a resume, researched opportunities, but almost as quickly as I readied myself for the workforce, I hit a brick wall.

The job market for my expertise (or lack thereof) was practically non-existent, unless I was willing to pack up my life and move halfway across the country. I was offered a full-time on-air meteorology position in Boulder Creek, Colorado. The catch? A starting salary of $17,500 a year in one of the most expensive places to live. Being close to my family and friends helped me decide to take a hard pass, again, lacking the foresight of what the opportunity may have led to.

At 23 years old, I found myself stuck. I was living at home, having fun with friends, and trying to make sense of what to do next. By the summer of 2004, things had really stalled. Odd jobs filled my time—one of which, briefly, was as a gas station attendant—and my social life became a bit too social. Casual drinking had gotten a bit too casual, and I found myself in a monotonous cycle of late nights and zero direction.

My father, the hardworking blue-collar business owner who had built his life from the ground up, had seen enough. The same day I started the gas station job, he pulled me off the shift and declared, "You're coming to work for me."

Now, let me say this: I love blue-collar work. It's how my work ethic manifested. My father's success as a business owner taught me the value of hard work, sacrifice, and grit. He had built a life for our family by grinding through the kind of work that makes the American Dream possible. And I am forever grateful for that.

But it sucked.

It might sound arrogant, but it was never supposed to be *my* life. I wasn't supposed to be in an exterminator truck, driving through the five boroughs of New York, battling rats and cockroaches in the blistering cold or unbearable heat from 7 a.m. to 4 p.m. My parents didn't want it for me, and I didn't want it for myself. They worked hard to ensure my siblings and I wouldn't have to take that path, and I had worked hard to honor their sacrifices and forge a different future.

But there I was. Two college degrees, a reservoir of ambition, and no prospects in sight. I was pounding the pavement as a laborer for $125 a day, stuck in a cycle of frustration which would eventually manifest to self-pity. For the first time in my life, I felt the weight of real disappointment. It was a humbling experience, one that left me questioning everything about where my life was headed.

Pride has never been a virtue I cling to, but I took pride in what I had accomplished. I had education, skills, and dreams—but none of it seemed to matter. That feeling came to a head on a sweltering August day in 2004. I was working for my dad, at a call for carpenter ants, probably still reeking of fun from the night before, when the homeowner opened her front door and greeted me with a cheerful, "Hello, how are you today?" My response, dripping with frustration and despair, was, "I'm a goddamn exterminator, lady. How the hell do you think I am?" *Oops.*

That moment was a snapshot of where I was, not where I wanted to be, but where I'd landed. It was a time in my life defined by disillusionment and desperation. Also, a time when I couldn't see past the next day, let alone envision a better future. But unbeknownst to me, it was also the first step on a path I never expected to take.

I wasn't supposed to be in an exterminator truck. I wasn't supposed to be lost and stuck. But those moments of despair were quietly pushing me toward something else I had never imagined. It wasn't where I thought I was headed, but it was where I needed to

5

WHAT'S HE DOING NOW?

Life has a way of surprising us. A chance meeting, a casual conversation—these seemingly insignificant moments can alter the course of our lives in ways we never could have imagined. Looking back, I can connect the dots to one such moment that set me on a path I never wanted to take: the path to being a teacher.

Growing up in a good community often means attending good schools with great teachers, and I was lucky to have both. Because I was curious about so many subjects, I always had a good rapport with my teachers. One subject I excelled in was Spanish.

For whatever reason, learning Spanish came naturally to me. Maybe I had an ear for it, or maybe it was my knack for dissecting words and understanding their meaning. From the start, I recognized the cognates and patterns of the language, and it all clicked. Whatever the reason, Spanish quickly became one of my best subjects, and my eighth-grade Spanish teacher, Mr. Zocchia, took notice.

As I progressed through high school, my Spanish skills only improved. By the time I heard about a school trip to Spain that Mr. Zocchia was organizing in the spring of 1998, I knew I had to go. I convinced my younger brother to come along, and we joined a group from the community for an unforgettable 10-day trip.

It was a transformative experience. Immersed in the culture and language, I felt like everything I had learned in the classroom was coming to life. And I think it was gratifying for Mr. Zocchia to see it, too. There I was, in the birthplace of the language he had taught me, confidently navigating the culture and speaking Spanish fluently.

A few years later, while I was busy with my day job as a "goddamn exterminator," Mr. Zocchia organized another school trip, this time to Italy. I didn't go, but my parents did, and during that trip, they became close friends with him. As they got to know each other, the inevitable question came up:

"What's Paul doing now?"

The truth was, I wasn't doing great. My parents, probably relieved to hear someone of influence express concern, were honest. I don't know how much they told him, but it was enough for him to come up with a suggestion that would change everything.

Mr Zocchia, who had become the director of personnel by then, offered up a suggestion: "Why doesn't Paul substitute for our school district while he looks for a job?"

When my parents brought up the idea, I laughed. Substitute teaching? Was that a joke? All I could think about were the antics we used to pull on substitute teachers when I was in school. The idea seemed absurd. But then reality hit me. I was 24 years old, going nowhere fast, spending too much time partying with friends and killing termites during the day. And I was going to scoff at this opportunity?

After some self-reflection, I realized I didn't have anything to lose. So I picked up the phone, called Mr. Zocchia and spoke to him, conceding to my reality, "Yes, I'll submit my resume on Monday and report to work on Tuesday. Thank you for the opportunity."

The following Tuesday, I found myself walking into my old elementary school, ready for my first day as a substitute teacher. I think I was more caught up in the excitement of starting something new than in the reality of what the job would entail. The idea of managing a classroom full of kids hadn't fully sunk in yet.

Little did I know that a casual conversation between my parents and Mr. Zocchia would set me on an entirely new course. I wasn't just starting a new job; I was stepping into a new chapter of my life. What began as a temporary solution to a rut would become the foundation for a career I never saw coming.

And so, with a mix of nerves, doubt, and a whole lot of curiosity, I started down a path I never wanted to take—the path to being a teacher.

6

I CAN'T DO THIS

That cool November morning, I walked into my old elementary school to substitute for a music teacher. As I entered the building, a flood of memories came rushing back. I was standing in the same classroom I had sat in as a primary school student, only now I was on the other side of the big desk. It was surreal.

The student desks looked impossibly small, the hallways seemed narrower, and everything about the building felt like a time capsule. Then there was the bathroom. Not realizing there was a faculty restroom, I found myself hunched over a child-sized urinal like John Candy in *Uncle Buck*.

"Gulp."

Despite the strangeness, I took on other substitute jobs in other elementary schools in town, and those first few months weren't so bad. Managing young kids for five hours a day was surprisingly effortless and straightforward. I packed my lunch, followed a structured schedule, collected a steady paycheck, and began to think, "Maybe I can do this after all."

But life has a way of humbling you when you least expect it.

The Call

I had just about settled into my new role as an elementary school teacher when one morning, at 4 a.m., my phone rang, as it always did when the district needed substitutes. Bleary-eyed, I answered, expecting another elementary school assignment.

"Hi Paul, we need you at the high school today. Report to the main office when you get there. Have a great day!"

"*Gulp.*"

The pit in my stomach was instant. "High school?" I thought. "I'm not ready for high school. They're going to chew me up and spit me out!"

As I drove up the familiar path to my old high school that morning, my nerves were in overdrive. My heart was pounding so hard it felt like it was echoing off the dashboard: *thump-thump, thump-thump*. I even half-jokingly thought about "accidentally" swerving off the road to avoid the whole ordeal.

You guessed it. "*Gulp.*"

When I got to the main office, they handed me my schedule. Of course, it wasn't an honors or life skills class, maybe something I could handle while I adapted to the new environment. No, I'd been assigned to a teacher who taught five classes of behavioral students—the kind of kids who lived to torment substitute teachers. Beggars can't be choosers, they say. So I was at the mercy of what was ahead of me. *Gulp.*

As I walked into the classroom, I could feel the chaos waiting to erupt. The bell rang, and the students were everywhere—standing, yelling, and swearing loudly enough that I could hear every word. Within minutes, they began shoving desks against the walls, throwing crumpled paper, and launching spitballs across the room.

"Okay, stay calm," I told myself. *Gulp.*

"Alright, everyone, take your seats. I'm Mr. Vecchione, subbing for Mrs. O'Brien today."

No response.

"Hey, everyone! Please sit down!"

Nothing. The room only got louder.

Then I spotted him—Matt A. He was sitting in the back, firing dry-erase markers across the room with the kind of accuracy that would've impressed the New York Mets.

I was a deer in headlights, lacking the ability or experience of how to speak to this kid in a way that would have diffused the situation. A sense of irony fell over me, as it was not too long ago that I was the one in the back of the room playfully harassing classmates to the dismay of substitute teachers. But there I was, the roles reversed, with absolutely no idea what to do. Looking back, the way I decided to handle it was probably the wrong way. But I was a stranger in a strange land. A rookie.

"What the hell are you doing?" I shouted as I marched toward him, my heart pounding louder with each step. *Thump-thump, thump-thump.*

Matt turned and glared at me with disdain. "What the fuck did you just say to me?"

"Gulp."

Every student in the room stopped and turned to watch. Matt stood up slowly, revealing that he was a full two inches taller than my 6'2" frame, with arms that looked like they belonged in a wrestling ring. He walked right up to me, our noses almost touching. My heart was pounding so loudly now I thought it might burst: *thump-thump, thump-thump, thump-thump.*

Again, with zero experience in this situation I said the only thing I could think of.

"Alright Matt, let's go to the office," I said, trying to keep my voice steady. It cracked anyway.

"I'm not going anywhere," he sneered.

"Gulp."

Expecting Matt to follow me out the door was quickly met with complete disillusionment. He was correct, he was not going anywhere, and he somehow even managed to get closer to me than he originally was. It was tantalizing.

He's going to take a swing, I thought.

I felt imminent danger, for sure, but I was fighting back my instinct to throw a protective first punch in a situation that was not going to end well for me. Matt got within a centimeter of my face, so close that I could smell the Mountain Dew on his breath. Our noses were nearly touching. *Thump..thump..* I am about to physically fight a student in my first class as a substitute teacher in my old high school. HOLY SHIT!

Well, this was fun while it lasted, but I've got to defend myself, I thought.

I would be lying if I said I remembered the exact words he spat in my face that day. I do know that we were eye to eye, in the middle of that classroom, with every student watching and heckling, about to go to blows. My guess is we had choice words, chock full of profanities and insults, but since I was supposed to be the authority figure, I couldn't bring myself to get physical with him until he acted first. But he didn't.

Matt backed down. To be clear, it was nothing that I did or said. I think he just thought the better of it and backed off. He left the classroom and went to the In-School Suspension room, somewhere, I reckon, he was used to being.

Exhale.

The crisis passed, but the uncertainty persisted, and a sliver of defeatism crept in. At the time, I was only 24, only 6 years older than the seniors in the school. I don't recall Matt's age, but his audacity to come toe to toe with me and the intensity behind his eyes as we stared each other down was so palpable that I was shaken to my core. Never had I ever expected to be in such a situation, at my first attempt to be an authority figure in a classroom full of high school students. I remember my ears feeling like they were on fire. It was a gut punch and a gut check.

The rest of the day, I just sat in the teacher's chair and made sure the kids didn't kill each other, which I succeeded at. But I didn't care because it was just survival at that point, and I knew it would be my last day as a substitute teacher at a high school, at least for a while.

Deflated, defeated, and angry, a lot of thoughts entered my mind that afternoon. *Was I crazy? This is not for me. I nearly killed or got killed on my first day on the job at a high school.*

I'm kidding myself!

I drove home from school that day with only one thought in mind, *I can't do this.*

The experience with Matt A. that morning left me in complete disbelief, not only by his actions but by my complete lack of experience in diffusing the situation. It also left me with a profoundly new respect for educators everywhere, particularly those in a high school setting.

But, despite all of this, and little did I know, it would be yet another instance that put me on a path that I never wanted to be on, the path to becoming a teacher.

Bringing Down the Temperature: A Teacher's First Real Test

Needless to say, after my experience with Matt A., I steered far clear of the high school for the rest of the fall semester in 2004. Just thinking about that day gave me flashbacks of heart-pounding chaos. *Gulp.* But now, as I reflect on it 20 years into my teaching career, I can't help but chuckle.

Sure, it's easy to laugh with the benefit of hindsight and the wisdom of experience. At the time, though, it was pure hell. Yet that day taught me my first real lesson about being a teacher—yes, even as a substitute: Your job, above all else, is to maintain the safety and security of the students in your classroom. First and foremost, you're there to bring the temperature down to a reasonable level so that learning (or at least survival) can happen.

On that infamous day with Matt A., I not only failed to lower the temperature but I was responsible for turning it into a full-blown inferno. It nearly derailed my teaching career before it even began. But was that the fault of a high school kid, or mine? Looking back, I know the answer. It was mine.

Kids will always be kids. They're unpredictable, sometimes wild, and often testing the limits just because they can. As a teacher, particularly as a substitute, you're walking into a room as an outsider, the natural adversary of their fun. Even the most unruly, unbalanced, or outright certifiably insane cherubs are still deserving of your best efforts to bring calm to the chaos. That's what I didn't understand at the time, but boy, did that experience teach me.

Had I faced the same situation today, it would have gone very differently. But as they say, hindsight is 20/20.

7

FINDING MY STRIDE

B y the fall of 2005, I had some solid experience as a substitute teacher under my belt. I had spent the remainder of the 2004 school year bouncing between classrooms at all grade levels (except high school, of course), slowly but surely finding my footing.

I began to settle into the role with relative ease, enjoying it. What had started as a stopgap job—a way to buy time before I pursued my dreams of being a writer, journalist, broadcaster, or meteorologist— was becoming something I could see myself doing long-term.

The interaction with the kids, the camaraderie with my colleagues, and the opportunities to coach, tutor, and develop relationships with students of all ages—it all started to click. I even ventured back into the high school level and, to my surprise, found a real connection with the older kids.

It turns out, I had a knack for relating to them, something I never could have imagined a year earlier. So, I thought, *why not?* Maybe being a full-time teacher wasn't such a scary idea after all.

Taking the Leap

After a few more months of subbing, I decided to pull the trigger. I enrolled in a teaching certification program and began working toward a second master's degree, this time in English and Special Education at the secondary level. It was late 2005, and like with my first master's, I put my head down and plowed through. By the end of 2006, I was a fully certified teacher, ready to start my career.

Now, I know this seems like a paradox. The title of this book is *I Never Wanted to Be a Teacher,* and up until that point, it was true. But here's the thing—it was convenient. It was seamless. And, in my naïve mind, it was just a stepping stone until "something else" came along.

Amazing how naïve we are when we're young. I still remember telling myself, *This isn't going to be my true profession. It's just a temporary gig—a steady job with a paycheck until I figure out what I really want to do.* Good plan, right? Nope.

I believe that things happen for a reason, even if we can't see it at the time. And little did I know, fate was about to show me just how wrong I was about teaching being "temporary."

Full Circle

After completing the coursework and a brief stint as a student teacher, I walked into the classroom again, this time as a full-time, probationary teacher, it was surreal. Not only was I starting my career as an English and Special Education teacher, but I was doing it at the very same high school I attended as a student (and nearly got taken out by Matt A. as a rookie substitute).

I can still feel the mix of nerves and excitement that accompanied me into that building. The minor leagues (subbing) were behind me. This is my career now. And somehow, even though I never wanted to be a teacher, I felt ready.

Or at least I thought I did. *Gulp.*

The next chapter of my life was about to begin, and I was walking straight into it. Teaching wasn't what I had envisioned for myself, but sometimes life's best plans are the ones you never saw coming.

Finn

The first ten years of my teaching career, with all its bumps and tribulations along the way, brought me lessons, relationships, and perspectives that only hands-on experience could provide. Among the many students I worked with, four (with pseudonyms) stand out above the rest—Finn, PJ, Ryan, and Parker. Each of them taught me something invaluable, but none more so than Finn.

Finn was one of the students in my first-ever teaching assignment. From the moment I met him, it was clear he had some significant challenges. He was a social outcast, carried a significant learning disability, struggled with personal hygiene, and had lost a parent at a young age. On top of all that, Finn was morbidly obese. He was, in many ways, a textbook example of a student who had every card in the deck stacked against him.

Yet, as I got to know Finn, it became clear that I could bring a little positivity into his world.

The Struggle

Finn had a hard time in school. Social situations were a nightmare for him. He wore stained shirts, his wiry hair was always disheveled, and the smell of unbrushed teeth lingered in the air. He sat in the back of the room, trying desperately to stay out of the crosshairs of his classmates' ridicule. But no matter how hard he tried to stay invisible, the bullying followed him like a shadow.

One day, it all came to a head.

I was circulating the classroom as part of my role as a special education co-teacher. It was my job to assist students who needed extra help, and I liked that I had the opportunity to work one-on-one with them. That day, I made my way toward the back of the room, where Finn sat.

The whispers and giggles had been bubbling under the surface all class, but when I approached Finn's desk, I saw him kicking a folded piece of paper toward me, trying to be as discreet as possible. I bent down and picked it up.

"FAT SMELLY FUCK, KILL YOURSELF."

I felt sick. My stomach churned as I looked at Finn and saw the pain in his eyes. It was a look that begged for help. But there was no way of knowing who had slipped Finn the note that day. Still inexperienced, I did the only thing I could think of.

I whispered to him, "Stay after class."

A Heartbreaking Conversation

When the bell rang, Finn stayed behind and told me everything. Through tears and gasping breaths, he poured out his life story—the loss he suffered as a child, his struggles with weight, his declining self-esteem, and the relentless bullying he endured daily.

It was devastating. As he spoke, he tried so hard to conceal his feelings, but couldn't. I knew I could relate to what he was feeling, albeit minimally. But the sting of ridicule aside, I gathered my thoughts and decided that this may have been too big for me. I couldn't fix this on my own, no matter how hard I tried. As a special education teacher, you learn quickly that there are support systems in place for students with disabilities. I wasn't entirely well-versed in how to access them, but I knew they were there.

"Finn, what are you doing to help yourself through this?" I asked gently.

He just shook his head and cried harder.

I couldn't let this go. I wasn't a mental health expert, but I knew I could at least connect him with the resources available in our school.

So that's what I did. I helped Finn find support through therapists and counselors, and though the systems in place weren't perfect, they gave him a space to talk about his struggles and begin to heal. Finn had been familiar with these support systems but hadn't taken advantage of them until I intervened. At that point, it was all I knew how to do.

Building a Connection

Finn, seeing the school psychologist weekly, began to come out of his malaise and also started visiting me during his free periods. He'd sit at my desk, often staring at the Sago Palm Tree plant I kept there, and tell me about his progress. He was working on his self-esteem, practicing better hygiene, and even taking small steps toward healthy habits. They were small and inconsistent steps, at first, but steps he was taking nonetheless. And I was relieved.

Over time, I saw a transformation in Finn. It wasn't perfect or immediate, but he started to hold his head a little higher. He began to laugh more and engage with the world around him. Eventually, he graduated from high school on time with his classmates and, after a long road, was strong enough to pursue life after high school.

"They won't always remember what you taught them, but they will never forget how you treated them."

During my time with Finn, I learned this most important lesson about teaching.

I don't know if I changed Finn's life, but I like to think I helped. What I do know is that my willingness to listen, empathize, and show him that he mattered gave him a flicker of light in a dark time.

We stayed in touch after he graduated. Occasionally, we'd grab coffee or lunch and talk about his college experiences and friends. Over the years, we lost touch, but now and then, I'd get a message from him— updates about his life, words of encouragement, and reminders of how much those days in high school meant to him.

When I asked Finn to write something for this book, he didn't hesitate:

> *Vex! (My nickname since I was a kid, short for Vecchione)*
>
> *I can only speak from planet Earth when I say this, but may the force be with you always. It's great to hear from you. When you told me you were writing a book about your teaching career, I thought about what you have meant to me in my life. You were always honest with me, so can I please be honest with you? Thanks.*
>
> *In high school, I thought you saved my life. There were some pretty*

dark days those years. I am positive that there were times I didn't want to stick around. This is hard for me to talk about, so I am glad my name will remain anonymous.

Anyway, after much thought, I realized that you did not save my life. Only I could do that. But what I could not give myself to be in the position to save my own life, you gave me.

I was pretty mixed up. I was blaming everyone else for my place in life. What you did do was change my attitude about life. You gave me hope every single day. I knew you were going to be sitting at your desk every morning, with that dumb pineapple plant! But you would be there, ready to just let me talk. You always gave me the best advice. And you taught me to love myself in a way I could never have imagined when I was a teenager. Anyway, it was the start of my reinvention for myself, and if you'll let me, I wish to thank you once again. When you reached out to me and asked if I would be willing to write you a letter to be published in your book, it made my whole day. You are the best, and thank you for all that you have done for me.

I wish you all the best of luck with your new book.
—Finn N.

Go figure—I never even wanted to be a teacher.

PJ

If Finn taught me the power of empathy and the importance of building meaningful relationships in my first year of teaching, PJ showed me the transformative impact of mentorship, resilience, and trust during my second year. The setting and circumstances were entirely different, but the lesson was just as profound: as a teacher, you might be the only positive adult presence in a student's life. That realization is both sobering and motivating.

Growing up, I had no shortage of love and support. My family was a solid unit that shaped who I am today. I didn't fully understand the meaning of "it takes a village" until much later, but my experience teaching PJ in the fall of 2007 planted the seed that would grow into a deeper understanding of how important that village is, especially for kids with so many struggles.

PJ was tall, thin, and lanky—a quiet kid who seemed to blend into the background by design. He rarely spoke or asked for help and had mastered the art of avoiding attention. Beneath that quiet exterior, however, PJ was struggling. As a ninth grader, he was reading at a fourth-grade level.

It would have been easy for him to slip through the cracks, especially since he didn't want to burden anyone with his struggles. But a chance conversation on an unusually warm November day changed everything.

PJ and I were seated in the back of Room 132, about to read through a test together. As we settled in, he glanced out the window.

"Warm out," PJ said.

"It is," I replied. "I wonder if it'll stay like this through the weekend?"

"Who cares," he muttered.

The tone caught me off guard. Thanksgiving weekend was approaching, and his words felt heavy.

"What do you mean?" I asked.

"I mean I don't care. Thanksgiving sucks."

I was stunned. Thanksgiving—food, football, family—was a holiday I associated with joy and togetherness. I'd never heard anyone describe it as something that "sucks." My first instinct was to let it go, but something about PJ's demeanor stopped me.

"Aren't you going to see family?" I asked gently.

"No. I don't have family, and my mom is working," he said matter-of-factly.

"Working? On Thanksgiving?"

"Yeah. She'll probably bring home McDonald's for dinner, but that's about it. My dad always says he'll come, but he never shows up."

His words hit me hard. There it was—everything about PJ's struggles, wrapped in a few sentences. But with the test in front of us, I had to put the conversation on hold.

"Okay, let's get through this test," I said, though the pit in my stomach remained.

Digging Deeper

I couldn't let it go. Something inside me needed to know more, so I started digging. What I found was difficult to endure.

PJ's mom was a single mother of four, working two jobs to provide for her family. They lived in a small apartment, scraping by day to day. PJ's dad, though idolized by his son, was absent. He made promises to visit but often left PJ waiting on the porch, looking down the street for someone who would never come.

Despite everything, PJ put on a good front. He wore new sneakers, nice clothes, and had a kind, amiable demeanor that made him well-liked by his peers. But it was all a façade, a way to hide his harsh reality.

Building Trust

At first, PJ was hesitant to let me in. I imagine he had significant trust issues, especially with adult men, and I couldn't blame him. But over time, he began to open up.

He started coming to my classroom before school, during lunch, and after class. Some days, we'd talk about sports—the Yankees, the Knicks, whatever was on his mind. Other days, our conversations were deeper, touching on his struggles at home and his challenges in school.

I tutored PJ in several subjects, often giving him writing prompts to help him express himself. Writing became a way for him to clear his mind and process his emotions. Slowly but surely, PJ began to find his voice.

Through our conversations, I realized how much my own experiences could help him. The lessons I'd learned from my trials and tribulations became tools I could share with PJ. He took my advice, applying it in ways that helped him navigate his difficult home life.

PJ passed all his courses and graduated on time with his peers—a triumph I'll never forget. Thanks to social media, I still keep in touch with him. Today, PJ is working full-time, living on his own, and doing well.

A Letter from PJ

When I asked PJ to write something for this book, his response was humbling:

Hey Mr. V,

How cool—you're writing a book! Thanks for letting me be a part of it. It's my pleasure to give your readers an idea of our experience when I was your student.

The best way I can describe my experience with you as my teacher is comfort. You always made me feel like I belonged. Your personality invited me into a world I wasn't always comfortable being in.

I think the book speaks for itself. You always seem to do things that are above and beyond to help others. I see your social media posts and all the great things you're doing, and I'm not the least bit surprised.

Thanks for always being there for me and showing me the way. I wouldn't be who I am today without you.

PJ

I know what you're thinking: "Wow, Paul, you're the greatest teacher ever!" *Cough, cough.* But here's the thing: I'm not. Teaching can be hard. It can be thankless, heartbreaking, and full of moments where you feel helpless.

But it's also the most rewarding in so many ways. PJ found a mentor in me, and I found a purpose in helping him. His story is a reminder that sometimes, all a kid needs is one adult who believes in them.

Some kids have stories and situations that are so terrible and that are so devoid of hope that it becomes overwhelming at times because the sad reality is that we can't help them all. But when you can help one, then another, then another, it validates everything you try to be.

What irony, because I never wanted to be a teacher.

Ryan

Let's talk about Ryan. I bring him into this story because he was, without a doubt, one of the most challenging students I've ever had in my 20 years of teaching. Ryan was likable, respectful, and self-aware about his struggles. He worked with me in the classroom and tried his best—when he wanted to. But, oh boy, could he be a pain in the ass. (And I say that with peace and love, my dude.)

Ryan will always be one of my all-time favorites, but getting to that point wasn't easy. Then again, what in life worth having comes easy? Especially in a profession like teaching—which, by the way, I never wanted to be a part of.

Ryan's home life was solid. He had both parents at home, a sister, a brother, and a comfortable middle-class life. His parents were involved in his education, passionate about ensuring he received the support he needed, and unafraid to get in your face if they thought you weren't pulling your weight. And I loved it. They reminded me of my own parents—people who demanded hard work, respect, and resilience while providing support and guidance along the way.

Ryan himself was outgoing, affable, and socially aware. He was athletic and played on the school's sports teams, but he had a severe learning disability. Reading, math, memory, organization—he struggled across the board. And while he was good-natured and cooperative most of the time, Ryan absolutely hated being redirected, told to try again, or challenged to do better. Pride, damaged self-esteem, and good old-fashioned teenage stubbornness created the perfect storm of resistance.

For a teacher like me, whose approach relies heavily on accountability, redirection, and encouragement, Ryan's personality tested my patience and creativity.

By Ryan's junior year, we'd been working together for over two years, and our dynamic was a bit like that of an older brother and younger brother. I challenged him to do better, and he resisted every step of the way. It was frustrating, to say the least, but also oddly rewarding.

That year, Ryan was busy with varsity sports, his first dabbles with dating, and the usual teenage distractions. Unfortunately, his academics began to suffer—particularly in English, which required a lot of writing. One essay assignment, in particular, was dense, comprehensive, and labor-intensive. Ryan barely put in any effort and bombed it, earning a 50.

I wasn't mad about the grade itself—failure happens. What infuriated me was his attitude and lack of effort. He had skipped our extra help session the day before, and when I approached him about it, things spiraled.

I walked up to his desk, scowling.

"Ryan, let's talk outside for a sec," I said.

"What? Why?" he replied, visibly annoyed.

"You know why. Let's go," I insisted.

He stood up, muttering under his breath—but not quietly enough.

"What the FUCK, guy?"

I froze. Did he just call me *guy*? After everything I'd done for him? The disrespect was infuriating.

"Excuse me?" I said, trying to keep my cool.

"I'm fucking done with this class, *guy*," he snapped.

Now I was seeing red—not the explosive kind I felt with Matt A. back in my first year, but the controlled, seasoned red that comes after years in the trenches. I ordered him out of the classroom, but before he could leave, I let him have it.

"Where do you get off talking to me like that?" I demanded. "Haven't I always been in your corner? Haven't I gone out of my way to help you? And this is how you talk to me?"

I laid into him, my voice trembling with frustration. By the time I was done, Ryan's tough-guy façade had completely crumbled. Tears streamed down his face, and he finally opened up.

"I'm beat, Vex. I'm shot," he choked out.

Breaking Down Walls

In that moment, Ryan let me into his world in a way he never had before. Between gasping sobs, he shared everything: the pressure from his parents, his academic struggles, his feelings of inadequacy on the ball field, and his shattered self-esteem.

"I'm a waste of skin," he said. "I'll never be anyone. I'll never be with a girl. Everyone laughs at me."

It was a gut punch. The mask of confidence and bravado he wore so well had completely fallen away, and I saw him for who he was—a struggling, overwhelmed kid who was drowning.

As I pondered the interaction Ryan and I had that day I couldn't help but think that maybe I was too harsh with him. Maybe controlling my emotions a little more would have spared Ryan what was without a doubt a low point in his life. And that wasn't my job. I was there to teach and encourage and mentor. Instead, I made a struggling student with disabilities ball his eyes out in embarrassment and shame.

But then it hit me. This was all true. My assessment was accurate but my perspective was flawed. What had come of it all? Yes Ryan was broken. Yes, Mr. Tough Guy was brought cascading back down to earth and yes he was belittled to the point of submission. None of which I was proud of but all of which needed to happen. Everything I was seeing with Ryan was a show. A mask to hide the inner struggles he was enduring and as it turned out, good old fashioned tough love was exactly what he needed.

I put a hand on his shoulder and let him talk. Sometimes, listening is more powerful than anything you could ever say.

Building the Village

The next day, I got to work. I met with the school psychologist, spoke to Ryan's parents, and connected with his other teachers and his coaches. Together, we built a plan: structured routines, clear goals, and regular communication to keep Ryan on track.

As it turns out, kids like structure. They need it and they flourish with it. Structure can be a lot of things. Routines, expectations, accountability, and structure can be the lifeline for kids, especially when they are drowning. Ryan was drowning. To help a teenager who is struggling, I also learned that it takes more than just a concerned teacher. It takes a collective effort.

Ryan responded to the structure immediately. He worked with a tutor for his academics, addressed some communication issues with his parents, and started rebuilding his confidence, step by step. It wasn't easy, but by the spring of his senior year, Ryan was back on track.

Teaching Ryan reminded me of one of the most important lessons in this profession: it truly takes a village. Family, teachers, coaches, and friends all play a role in helping a struggling student find their way. And when that village comes together, amazing things can happen.

Ryan graduated on time, found a great union job, and is thriving to this day. When I asked him to contribute to this story, he didn't hesitate:

Vex,

> *Thank you so much for letting me in on your book. I knew you would write a book one day. I'm really happy for you. Thank you for all that you've done for me. I was messed up in high school, but you were always*

the steady hand. I will never forget our talks. Even when I was an asshole, you never lost your faith in me. I loved being in your class.

Good luck with the book!

Ryan

Ah yes, I never even wanted to be a teacher.

Parker

In the teaching profession, no two days are ever the same. Students' moods, home lives, challenges, and triumphs shift constantly, creating an ever-changing landscape for educators to navigate. It's a delicate dance—balancing butterflies and lightning bolts while trying to foster a stable, productive, and fun classroom environment.

Some days, you're thrown challenges that test everything you think you know. On others, you're reminded of why you show up in the first place: to help kids. Parker, a short, spunky, spitfire of a student, was one of those reminders.

From the moment he walked into my classroom in the fall of 2008, I knew Parker would be a challenge. But I couldn't wait to meet it. The irony isn't lost on me—after all, I never wanted to be a teacher.

Parker faced challenges most students couldn't fathom. He was born with multiple birth defects, and a learning disability. High school is hard enough for "normal" kids; for someone like Parker, I couldn't imagine the daily battles he faced.

Yet when he walked into my classroom for the first time, Parker immediately defied every expectation.

"Hello, I'm Parker. Who are you?" he said with surprising confidence.

"I'm Mr. Vecchione, Parker. It's nice to meet you."

"Likewise," he said, a mischievous glint in his eye.

It was clear from the start that Parker's way of coping with his struggles was humor.

"So, what's first? A shoelace around my wrist and a kick in the ass to see what I can do?" he said, grinning.

I nearly spat out the mouthful of coffee I'd just taken. He said it so casually, with perfect comedic timing. The whole room burst into laughter, and in that moment, all I could do was laugh myself. Humor was his armor—a way to redirect attention from his physical and academic challenges and command the room on his terms, and for that, I had to respect him.

Parker and I crossed paths throughout his entire high school career. Whether by chance or design (likely both, thanks to his parents), he ended up in my class—or at least in my orbit—year after year.

Despite his disabilities, Parker approached every challenge with determination. If he struggled, he'd ask for help. If he didn't, he'd put his head down and get the job done.

One day, during Regents exam season, Parker came to my classroom for extra help. After we finished reviewing, he surprised me with a question.

"Do you like your job, Mr. V.?"

"I do, most of the time," I replied.

"Why?" he asked.

"That's a loaded question," I said, smiling. "There are so many reasons, but I tell all my students this: aside from helping kids and shaping the future, it keeps me young."

"What the hell does that mean?" he shot back, his trademark sarcasm on display.

"It means I never wanted to be a teacher," I admitted. "But I never wanted to grow up, either. Teaching lets me spend time with teenagers, connect with them, and, sometimes, act like I'm 17 again."

Parker laughed, but then he said something that stopped me in my tracks.

"Funny, you don't strike me as a typical teacher," he said.

"Oh?" I asked, curious.

"Nah. Most of my teachers are great. They focus on curriculum and make class fun. But you give off this vibe—like you're one of us. A lot of my friends think so too. It makes things a bit less stressful. Never change that."

It was awesome. Here's a kid whose every moment of life is chock-full of challenges, telling me how it is. Parker had just described what made me a good teacher, and he'd done so with the wisdom and conviction of someone far beyond his years. I wasn't expecting it, but who was I to argue? *Ha!*

The Gift of Struggle

Parker's self-assurance wasn't something he developed on his own. It was the result of years of intentional effort by his parents, as I learned during a parent-teacher conference one October evening.

"Parker carries himself with such confidence," I told his mom. "How did you help him get there?"

Her response was unforgettable.

"We knew early on that Parker would struggle," she said. "But we also knew that struggle is a gift. It shapes you. It makes you who you are."

She went on to explain how they'd instilled in Parker the belief that he was no different than anyone else—and that his struggles didn't define him. Instead, they were opportunities to grow stronger.

Parker's parents were the support system he needed at home, and they taught him the importance of the gift of struggle. It compelled him to use his weaknesses as a source of strength, and it was on full display every day.

A Lesson in Confidence

Parker's story is a testament to the power of resilience, the importance of a strong support system, and the transformative impact of education. He reminded me that confidence can be cultivated and that, sometimes, the greatest lessons come from the students themselves.

Parker had a support system in place that made his situation not only manageable but a crucial life lesson for someone who would have almost no chance without it. It was so satisfying to witness, and it even restored some of my faith in humanity. Not only did he need the support, he received it, it was ingrained in his persona and his psyche and his gait, and it rubbed off on me. Parker taught me, albeit inadvertently, that confidence is a virtue, and it is within reach of anyone with the right support system. His parents were it. And they leaned on Parker's teachers for reinforcement. Which I was happy to provide. If Parker embodied confidence, his parents embodied the type of strong moral values some kids lack today. Because it wasn't arrogance or entitlement, it was: *I am who I am, and nothing will stop me.* All this from a severely disabled kid who was determined not to let his shortcomings define him: quite the opposite. It was refreshing to witness and a blessing to be a part of. Confidence is a virtue, no matter who you are and what forces are against you. Yeah, that is something I can hold onto as I reflect on my time with Parker.

A Letter from Parker

Parker graciously contributed to this book with a letter that encapsulates his journey:

Dear Mr. Vecchione,

This is really cool, but I don't know what to say. I wish I were better at writing than I am.

It's easy to say what you've meant to me in my life. I thought I had everything figured out every day, but I know now that wasn't the case — and you were always there to help me find my way.

Even though I have some teachers in my family, I don't think any of them measure up to you. You are real, and you have expectations, but I was never afraid to make a mistake in your class.

I hope your students today know how lucky they are to have you.

Parker

All of my students carry a certain memory in my mind. I am extremely grateful and consider myself very lucky to have the opportunity to interact with and shape individuals in my classroom. Teaching isn't for everyone. There are certain aspects and twists and turns that make it one of the most difficult professions in the world. But it is also the most rewarding. I can go on with anecdotes and letters from students for a very long time, but it was these first several students who have left an indelible mark on my career as an educator.

There's that irony again—I never even wanted to be a teacher.

As I entered the second decade of my teaching career, the twists and turns were omnipresent, it's the nature of the beast. Any time you work in the public domain with teenagers, there is never going to be complete tranquility, 100% of the time. This makes the profession challenging but fun at the same time, because we have to always be on our toes, with different scenarios and situations flying at us at any given time. It can be exciting and grueling at the same time. Real time problem solving, the pressures from above to perform at our best and adhere to the seemingly endless new rules and procedures, and regulations, students, parents, colleagues, and on and on. I am not exaggerating when I say that education may be among the most difficult professions. But that second decade, around 2010 or so, forces within the universe would coalesce around me and bring unforeseen challenges that would shape my career and my personal life forever.

PART II

DUELING CRISES

8

THE STIGMA

In the United States, the stigma surrounding mental illness is, and has always been real. Growing up, we rarely heard the term "mental illness" unless it was concerning something or someone significant. Jeffrey Dahmer, who killed young boys and ate their corpses. Ted Bundy, who stalked young women, raped them, then beat them to death. John Wayne Gacey, who raped and murdered young boys and buried them under his house. Each of these stories came to light during the 1980s, and rightfully so, there was the general sentiment among the population that these serial killers were incredibly disturbed, deranged, homicidal, but complete outliers.

If notorious serial killers were out there, they were not in our community, and they were just insane; nothing to worry about. This was the 1980s, and the only time we heard of such horrors that we quickly attributed to mental illness. As far as I knew, it was only these extreme circumstances that mental illness could be equated with. Everyone else, except for a select few, did not suffer from mental illness. Sure, there were always those within your immediate sphere whom you wondered about, even heard about once in a while, who may be a bit unstable, but mostly they were okay. I remember a classmate and friend who, once in a while, would be called out of class to visit the school psychologist. He was from a broken family and sometimes had anger issues, but again, this was the extent of what the term mental illness might mean for us while growing up.

———

Fast forward to 2025, and we now know just how widespread and how extensive the so-called "mental illness" umbrella stretches. It's everywhere, and it impacts far more people than we ever thought possible. There has been considerable debate regarding the genesis of the current mental health crisis. But what is known is that for decades in the United States, mental health and its accompanying comorbidities have been stigmatized, marginalized, cast aside, and even flat-out ignored by the vast majority of people in this country. As we will learn, this would have devastating consequences on our society, families, communities, and children.

Spring 2010

I often wonder if everyone spends as much time reflecting on the past as I do. My mind is like a high-definition reel, always recording, capturing the most intricate details of moments long gone. It's both a gift and a curse. On one hand, my ability to recall exact conversations, weather conditions, clothing choices, and even subtle tones of voice amazes friends and family. On the other hand, this relentless memory can trap me in loops of rumination, replaying the past with a clarity that isn't always welcome. As I reflect, certain moments play on repeat in my mind, and one particular day stands out to me as vivid as if it happened yesterday—a chilly Sunday in March 2010, the first full day of spring. March 21st, to be exact.

A Sunday UnLike Any Other

The day unfolded as Sundays often did. I was at my childhood home, surrounded by family. With two parents, three siblings, their spouses, several young kids, and two excitable Boston Terriers, the house was a constant swirl of noise, laughter, mild arguments, and chaos. It was a welcome madness, but after a while, it could feel suffocating.

Shoeless and coatless, I stepped out onto our old wooden deck, which was weathered by years of wear, so much so that the boards creaked under your feet as you walked. The air still carried the chill of winter, sharp and refreshing. I sat down on the higher of the two leveled decks, next to the hot tub, taking deep breaths of the brisk air, letting it ground me.

Then came the buzz of a text message in my pocket. I pulled out my phone and saw the name: *Kerrie C.*

Kerrie was a former student and softball player of mine. We'd kept in touch since her graduation the year before, exchanging occasional texts about life and sports. But this was unusual—it wasn't like Kerrie to text on a Sunday afternoon. Curious, I opened the message.

"Someone in my grade committed suicide this weekend."

Gut punch.

"Huh?" I texted back, confused and horrified.

"She hung herself in her closet over the weekend."

I stared at the screen in disbelief. "Oh my God," I replied, struggling to find words.

A New Reality

Teen suicide wasn't on my radar—at least, not like this. In my 34 years as a resident and educator in my community, nothing like this had ever happened. It was unthinkable.

Kerrie didn't share many details, and I didn't press her. I didn't know the girl who had died. She wasn't my student or one of the players I coached. But the news sent shockwaves through our small suburban community. Rumors began swirling—whispers about bullying, social media, and a toxic online environment that may have played a role.

At the time, social media was exploding. Platforms like My Space and Facebook had become a central part of teenagers' lives, creating a space where interactions were instantaneous, far-reaching, and often anonymous. The potential for bullying was amplified, constant, omnipresent, and inescapable.

What had started as a way to connect with friends and family had become a breeding ground for cruelty. And in 2010, we were just beginning to understand the consequences.

The morning after learning of the suicide of a teen in our school, I walked into the building with a heavy heart. Our principal had called an emergency faculty meeting before the start of classes.

The atmosphere in the auditorium was somber. Teachers and staff sat in silence, the weight of the tragedy palpable. Quiet sniffles punctuated the stillness as colleagues waited anxiously for answers.

The principal spoke briefly but with solemnity. Grief counselors would be available for students and staff. Teachers were urged to be sensitive and to send any visibly distressed students to the counseling office. The message was clear: tread lightly; these kids had just lost a friend.

The meeting ended, and we filed out to face the day. But the truth was, no one really knew what to do. For many of us, this was the first time we'd dealt with such a tragedy so close to home. Even our administration, despite its best intentions, seemed caught off guard.

In hindsight, the school's response was appropriate for the time, when teen suicide was not on the radar. A brief meeting, some grief counselors, and a reminder to be sensitive—was about the protocol because at the time, no one had a roadmap for navigating the shock and devastation of a tragedy that hit so close to home. It was unspeakable, but at the time, most chalked it up to an anomaly in our otherwise relatively quiet suburban community.

But for me, that day marked the beginning of a slow awakening. It was the first time I truly grappled with the enormity of mental health issues among teens. The questions haunted me: *What would drive a young girl, in the prime of her life, to end it all? Was this preventable? Were there signs that were missed?*

It was definitely a turning point—not just for our community, but for me. It was my first glimpse into the pervasive and often hidden struggles of mental illness, the devastating impact of bullying, and the urgent need for better support systems, particularly for teens, all issues that were coming to light not just in our community, but around the entire country.

This was the moment I began to see the cracks in the foundation—the gaps in how we, as educators and a society, address mental health. It planted the seed of what would eventually grow into my mission to bring awareness, education, and resources to the forefront.

But on that day in March 2010, all I could feel was the weight of loss and the faint stirrings of a purpose I hadn't yet discovered.

9

THE RUN

It is always the words of parents who have lost children to drug overdoses or suicide that haunt me the most. Their pain is profound, their voices heavy with grief and searching for strength. I had no idea the power of their words—until I heard them spoken in person, one-on-one.

One such parent was Barbara Sena, and I met her on an unseasonably warm Sunday morning in October 2017. It was at the annual Michael Sena Memorial Run For Hope, held at a local high school on Long Island. At the time, I was helping my closest childhood friend, Tim Sini, during his campaign for local elected office. This 5K was just another campaign stop on the schedule—or so I thought. What happened that day would become one of the most transformative experiences of my life.

As we arrived at the event, the air was alive with activity. Runners gathered at the starting line, vendors set up their tables, and music played from a stage in the distance. I knew this wasn't a typical community event, but the scene was full of energy and camaraderie.

After the runners took off, I wandered toward the other side of the field. That's when I saw them—a line of pickets stretching along the runners' path. Each picket displayed a photo, a name, an age, and a brief story.

At first, I didn't grasp what I was looking at. But as I got closer, it became clear. These were the faces of drug overdose victims.

Fourteen years old. Fifteen years old. Sixteen years old. Over and over, the same story repeated with different names and photos. There must have been a hundred pickets.

My stomach churned as I read each one. Their faces stared back at me —smiling in Halloween costumes, first communion suits, middle school graduation gowns. They were memories frozen in time.

I walked slowly with a heavy heart. Parents and family members stood nearby, some cheerful and others silent, their grief palpable. It felt like walking through the valley of the shadow of death.

A Nation in Crisis

By 2017, I was aware of the opioid epidemic ravaging the country, but it had always been a distant problem—something I read about in newspapers or saw on TV. That day, it became personal.

Children. These were children, kids with backpacks, birthdays and bicycles. Kids who should have been laughing, dreaming, and planning their futures. Instead, they had become victims of a crisis spiraling out of control.

The numbers were staggering. At the time, America was losing over 200 people a day to opioid overdoses. Most were in their adolescent years. How had we let this happen?

The 5K was an event to remember victims and serve as a platform for their families to share their stories. As the runners returned and gathered at the finish line, the day's speakers began addressing the crowd. Among them was Barbara Sena.

Barbara was the mother of Michael Sena, the young man for whom the event was named. She was soft-spoken yet commanding, her words resonating with everyone in attendance. She thanked each person individually, acknowledging their presence and support.

Her poise was remarkable. I couldn't imagine the strength it took to stand on that stage, reliving her pain to bring awareness to others.

Eventually, I had the chance to speak with Barbara one-on-one. She shared her story with me—Michael's story.

Michael Sena

Mother of an Addict – Michael's Story

On November 8, 2016, shortly before 6 a.m., not sleeping well, intuitively knowing something was wrong, I heard a knock at the door. It was a Suffolk County police officer. He asked me if I was Barbara Sena and proceeded to say, "I am sorry to inform you that your son, Michael Sena, is dead."

"What? How?"

I fell to the ground, screaming. "No. No, please, God, no!"

The first person I called was my eldest son, Tommy. The police officer had to speak because nothing came out of my mouth except screams. A lot of blur, but my next vivid memory was my daughter, Nikki, screaming and crying, throwing her hands on the floor, with my friends holding her, crying.

My son Michael lived in Florida at that time, about 45 minutes from Tommy. Tommy had to identify the body. How horrible to imagine having to identify your dead younger brother's body.

Let us start from the beginning.

On October 28, 1990, Michael Paul Sena was born—the second son of Barbara and Paul. Michael was a great friend with a wonderful sense of humor, a contagious laugh, and an infectious smile. He was a natural athlete who excelled at sports and was a loving and caring individual to anyone he crossed paths with. In high school, he was nominated for Homecoming King (took second), Most Athletic, and Most School-Spirited. Track, swimming, and most of all, football—playing both sides, safety, and running back—were some of his favorites.

I know he was not an angel. I did know he and his friends liked to drink alcohol. I thought if I knew about it, I could control it.

In October of 2009, Michael got a DWI. By the time we went to trial, he was twenty. They switched him over to Suffolk County Drug Court. After that, Michael started experimenting with Oxycodone pills. The experimenting quickly spiraled into a dependence on the drug. Like so many people who start in this way, this became an expensive habit that led to a dependence on heroin.

Michael got caught trying to pawn some of my jewelry with a fake ID. When he was brought back to my house, the police officer said, "Your son is on drugs. Look at his eyes; they are dilated."

As a parent, it is hard to fathom that your child would ever become a drug addict. This can happen to any of us. Do not be blind to the signs. Until you are involved with a family member who is an addict, you don't understand that this affects the whole family, not just your loved one.

This was the beginning of a journey that Michael and our family were about to take, in and out of rehabilitation facilities.

The first rehab was in upstate NY—28 days at Villa Veritas. Our insurance would only cover one inpatient rehab. At a parents' group, I distinctly remember a woman grabbing my arm and saying, "28 days is not enough!"

Oh boy, was she right.

Oh yes, and that was one and done with the insurance company.

Michael had a difficult time transitioning back into the real world. He came back and was a lifeguard over the summer, which he had done for many years. Once again, I knew something was off.

Did you know there is something called seasonal depression?

I did not!

Of course, that was one of Michael's issues.

At this point, he dropped out of college, was kicked out of the first trade school, and was using again!

Begging for help, not knowing where to turn, and insurance refusing to cover him, I found a place in Minnesota.

Thank you, Mom!

She lent me the money, and he was accepted into the facility. That is where he spent his 21st birthday. Sad, isn't it?

He was a star in these rehabs.

He came back and had to go into outpatient treatment. Oh yes, I had to pay out of pocket. Someone told me to get him on Medicaid and off my insurance. That is what we did.

Michael again had a hard time transitioning back into the real world.

Next stop—Daytop Village for IOP (Intensive Outpatient).

IOP failed, and he went back to inpatient at Daytop.

Once again, Michael was a star pupil.

He was a team leader.

He was allowed to escort people down to social services and the court.

But he was also learning terrible things—meeting up with dealers and how to deceive.

Michael graduated from that program.

What is a mom to do but bring your child home?

They tell you tough love.

No parent wants to see their child on the street, cold and hungry.

Michael was part of the Suffolk County Drug Court. If you tested clean every time you appeared, you were good.

Michael was working with a moving company. We thought he was doing well.

Many of his old friends and family didn't want to go near him.

The stigma is a real thing, even when you are clean.

I was always told, "He does not look like an addict."

My son never asked to be an addict.

I started doing more research and taking classes, only to find out that addiction is 95% genetic.

Yes, we have an addiction that runs in the family. Alcoholism is an addiction, too!

I brought Michael back to drug court. He looked so handsome in his suit and tie. I remember him sweating and panicking a bit.

When they called his name, he stood up and said,

"I failed the drug test—heroin."

I screamed and started hitting him from behind.

"How can you do this?"

They were going to throw me out if I did not stop.

I saw them handcuff him.

Through his tears, he kept saying, "I'm sorry, Mom. I'm sorry."

Michael had to detox in jail.

He told me it feels like you are dying.

I had to find him a court-approved facility within thirteen days, or he would have to stay in jail.

I found a facility past Albany (by the Canadian border) for 90 days.

Would this be long enough?

God bless Mom again.

We picked him up at the Riverhead jail at the crack of dawn.

If he was not there by 3 p.m., they would not take him.

He was so quiet the entire trip up.

When we stopped at a rest stop, he showed me his arms.

Oh my God! The track marks.

He looked so sad and defeated.

And said, "I'm sorry."

My daughter, Nikki, and I went up for a family visit. During this weekend, he shared with us that he had overdosed a few months before and was revived by Narcan.

A punch to the gut.

He also told me that doing heroin was euphoric.

Wow.

What do you say to that?

This is what family weekend is about—sharing the ugly side of addiction.

I feared that when the three months were up, it would be his death sentence if they did not keep him.

To my surprise, he went into a sober house and was the old Mike again.

He focused on his sobriety.

He ran 5 Ks, 10 Ks, and even a half marathon, including the Nassau County Marathon, running it in just under four hours.

This is when he said,

"I want to have a Run for Sobriety. I want to help others struggling and let them know it is possible to be happy and sober!"

That was one of our longest sober times with Mike—about 18 months.

I also realized running was an addiction for him.

He worked out all the time.

The kid had 8-pack abs.

During this sober time, he met his girlfriend.

She was amazed at how he was able to turn himself around and help others become sober.

He inspired so many!

At this point, Medicaid kicked him off, stating he could be self-sufficient now.

I had to put him back on my insurance.

He was still under 26, with no job or any real skills, and I let him live back home until he figured out his next steps.

Remember, I told you Michael did not do well transitioning back to the real world?

Now it was fall, and his seasonal depression was starting again.

He had a new job that required him to drive all over the place, and he was struggling.

Thinking he could just use a little bit of drugs to help him get through, he quickly realized he had a problem again.

His girlfriend and I helped him detox at home.

When that horror was over, I brought him to another facility, Seafield.

Ready to go back into an inpatient facility, he was denied.

He did not fail the drug test. He was clean.

Denied by the insurance company!

Michael said to me,

"Mom, I got this. I will go into the sober house in Riverhead and do IOP."

It was early January 2015.

I received a phone call in the middle of the night from the sober house —Michael had overdosed and was revived with Narcan.

He was at Peconic Bay Hospital.

I asked the house manager, "How?"

He told me, "Lady, I can't watch all these guys. I have no idea!"

In an impending blizzard, Nikki and I drove out there.

Michael wouldn't even look at me.

The hospital told me they were releasing him.

I begged them not to.

"He's a drug addict—what do you want us to do with him?"

Addiction is a disease.

If he had cancer, heart disease, or any other medical condition, they would have helped!

But not this.

Back home we went.

A False Hope

Silly me, not knowing what to do, I heard a commercial on the radio.

"If your loved one is struggling with addiction, we can help."

I thought it was a message from God.

Idiot!

It was a patient broker—someone who makes money by placing addicts in rehabs.

Off to Texas he went.

Star pupil again.

True leader and inspiration to others.

This time, they put him on Vivitrol—a drug that inhibits the urge to use.

I thought it was a bad idea.

If he used heroin, he wouldn't feel the effects, which meant he could overdose easily.

Home again!

He worked in landscaping now.

Then he was introduced to crack.

Heroin makes you nod off and lethargic.

Crack makes you pure evil and agitated.

Within a few months, he was spinning out of control.

Kicking him out.

Paying off dealers.

Buying back my stuff from pawn shops.

He was homeless.

I thought this was his rock bottom.

I guess rock bottom is different for everyone.

I called the rehab patient broker again.

This time, off to Florida in the fall of 2015.

They brought him to a facility with high spikes fences.

They still don't know how he escaped.

They called him Spider-Man.

Missing.

My family and I feared the worst.

I went down to Florida, and my son Tommy and I searched for Michael.

We checked the morgue.

We searched the alleys where the homeless stayed.

I started to lose hope.

Michael had a cell phone that only worked with Wi-Fi.

Finally, he called me from a Starbucks, begging for help.

My dad went down to find him.

Michael tried to kill himself, but the branch broke.

My father was able to bring him back to detox.

His organs were close to shutting down.

He was in the hospital for over a week.

They ended up placing him in a facility in Lake Worth, Florida.

Once again, he was their star pupil.

Christmas 2015 – A Mother's Promise

It was Christmas 2015, and Michael wanted to come home.

I told him, "I'm not ready."

I promised him next year.

(A promise I was never able to keep.)

I told him, "Keep up the good work."

He was running again, working out, and making amends—one of the 12 steps—with all those he had hurt.

We had our first family vacation in years—Disney.

He was amazing!

We had so much fun.

When we were leaving, Nikki started crying.

She said, "This is our last vacation together."

Michael was doing great.

We saw him again in September 2016.

We planned to all meet for Thanksgiving in Florida that year, since both my sons were living there.

Michael told us he wanted to move out of the sober house.

It was across the street from drug dealers, and he wanted to get out of there.

He didn't want to move back to Long Island because there were too many triggers.

The Final Days

- October 21: He moved into his apartment and celebrated one year of sobriety.

- October 22: He was rebaptized in the Christian religion.

- October 28: He celebrated his 26th birthday. I sent his girlfriend down to be with him, knowing the family was coming the following month.

- October 28: He was kicked off my insurance.

- November 4: He didn't get the job at the rehab. Everyone was dying from fentanyl-laced heroin.

- November 5: I was on the phone with Michael for about an hour. He was so upset about the job. He was on a break with his girlfriend, rent was due, and he had a cavity but no insurance.

- I promised I would help him.
    - He was too far from his support community.
    - He promised me he wouldn't touch heroin and told me, "I love you."
    - These were all triggers.

- November 6: The New Orleans Saints (his favorite team) lost that night. I texted him saying, "I am proud of you, and don't worry about the loss."

- November 7: I was calling and texting—no response.

- My other kids always tell me I can be annoying and that people are busy and can't always answer the phone.

The Moment That Changed Everything

On November 8, 2016, shortly before 6 a.m., I woke up with a feeling of dread.

Then came the knock at the door.

Michael didn't touch heroin—it was cocaine laced with fentanyl.

Saying Goodbye

We held the funeral in Deer Park that weekend.

I have never seen so many people in my life.

The receiving line was endless.

You could have told me you were there and weren't—I wouldn't have remembered.

We buried Michael in his Drew Brees New Orleans Saints jersey—his favorite player, his idol.

He looked so peaceful and still.

That night, we lit the sky with Chinese lanterns.

He would have loved that.

The Reality of Grief

Now, at the holidays, I visit him at St. Charles Cemetery.

I decorate his gravesite with seasonal themes.

We had the Trinity symbol etched into his headstone. It's a symbol that has always been important to our family.

When Tommy turned 18, he had a tattoo drawn with the Trinity symbol, which meant that the three siblings would always be connected.

I don't know if Michael had a premonition, but while in rehab, he drew tattoos.

One of them had the Trinity symbol with my kids' first initials surrounded by angel wings.

We all have that tattoo now.

It is also the symbol for the Michael Sena Run for Hope.

Turning Pain Into Purpose

At the funeral, I made it known:

"I want to honor Michael's legacy. We need to have a Run for Sobriety!"

This was the beginning of Michael Sena's Run for Hope.

I wanted to turn my pain into purpose.

I needed to make a difference and effect change.

My family and I did not want to see another family suffer such a tragic loss.

The United States was, and still is, at epidemic proportions, and there was not enough help then.

Now, there are more resources than ever before.

I now belong to the club that no parent ever wants to belong to—Angel Parents.

At the first annual Michael Sena's Run for Hope in October 2017, we made our mission clear:

We aim to inspire hope for individuals and families impacted by drug addiction by sharing knowledge and resources to:

- Raise awareness about drug abuse to prevent individuals from ever starting.
- Assist those battling addiction in finding the right resources to get sober.
- Support those in recovery by helping them find the right tools for a permanent, sober, and healthy lifestyle.

A Mother's Love Never Ends

My beautiful boy is no longer here on earth to share in the joy of his beautiful growing family or to experience his own life and family.

He had a zest for life and adventure.

It was cut way too short.

I miss him every single day.

A piece of my heart will always be missing.

Don't be blind.

Empower yourself with the right tools and knowledge.

Make sure your children are safe.

Teach them to never start using drugs of any kind.

A Final Message – In His Own Words

I will not be quiet.

These few pages are only glimpses into the past that I share with you.

There is so much more.

I leave you with a poem Michael wrote at one of the facilities.

There is so much pain and power in these words.

Be an advocate. Be smart.

FAREWELL TO MY ADDICTION

I'm afraid to take a left when I should have moved right.
It could have cost me my last breath and shown me my last
    night.
I never thought that I would die as a man of shame and guilt.
It brings tears to my eyes to think of what I built.
I was young and full of hope; I had a lot to give.
Then, after meeting Dope, I thought I didn't deserve to live.
I look at my reflection, and I think of what I see.
I have found a big connection with why I don't love me.
I thought that getting high was fun, but that is just insane.
Now all I do is run from my thoughts and all my pain.
It hurts me to look back, to dig into my past.
I know that for a fact, this life will never last.
Dope was my best friend, but it didn't love me back.
Now my heart will have to mend because it's full of breaks and
    cracks.
I gave you all my money, and I gave you all my love,

But there is nothing funny about losing all the above.
My loved ones hate my guts; they think that I am bad.
Best friend, you drove me nuts; you took everything I had.
I want all of that stuff back. Why won't you just let me go?
I'm on a brand-new track, only this time it's moving slow.
No more running fast and no more going hard.
I want you in my past because of you, I have been scarred.
Now that I can see how I cared and what we've done,
I'm ready to be free. I'm not scared. I will not run.
You're no longer my best friend. To that, I promise to be true.
This letter is the end of my relationship with you.

— MICHAEL SENA

A Promise to Keep Fighting

This is why I fight.

For Michael.

For every child, sibling, friend, and loved one who has been lost to addiction.

For every parent, sibling, and friend left behind, grieving.

For every person still fighting for their life.

If Michael were here today, I know he would still want to help others.

And that's exactly what I will do.

Lighting a Fire

After the run, I came home a different person. I sat with my thoughts, replaying the day over and over. As a parent myself, the idea of losing a child was unbearable. From the moment my first child was born, my entire world shifted.

Parenthood is a role that defies explanation. It's all-encompassing. You want to give your children everything—love, safety, happiness, and opportunities to thrive. You'll do anything to protect them from harm. The thought of the unthinkable, of losing them to drug overdose, was inconceivable.

But it was happening—every day, in communities just like mine. And reality began to set in--the opioid crisis wasn't a distant problem; it was here, in our backyard, stealing the lives of our children.

As I reflected on the Michael Sena Memorial 5K, I realized that something had to change. Barbara's words, the photos on those pickets, the stories behind them—they haunted me. But they also lit a fire.

Where have we gone wrong as a society? How had we allowed this epidemic to reach such devastating proportions? More importantly, what could we do to stop it?

That day marked the beginning of a journey for me—a commitment to learn, to advocate, and to act. It was no longer enough to be aware of the problem. I had to be part of the solution. I resigned myself to the fact that I was only one person. Yet I had experience with teenagers, with education, and with turning on a small light in a dark room for some of my students. I knew the task would be monumental, but I also knew that if I could help just one teenager stray off the path of the unthinkable, it would be worth the struggle.

Barbara's strength and resilience inspired me. She turned her grief into a force for good, and I knew I had to do the same. It wouldn't be easy, but for the sake of our children, it was necessary.

That day, I made a decision: I would be a part of the efforts to curb this crisis. And that decision would ultimately lead me to where I am today, standing at the forefront of a movement to protect and empower our kids. I can't fully explain it, but a fire was lit, and I would be damned if I let that fire burn out.

10

THE DEVASTATING FACTS

The stories of Michael Sena and the countless other children lost to overdose or struggling with mental health challenges are not isolated tragedies; they are symptoms of a broader, systemic crisis. These heartbreaking moments—the faces on the pickets, the quiet courage of grieving parents, the statistics that paint an increasingly dire picture—underscore a truth that can no longer be ignored. The United States, and communities everywhere, are facing the worst mental health and opioid crises in the nation's history, crises that demand action, understanding, and a willingness to confront uncomfortable realities. To fully grasp the scope of what we're up against, we must look beyond the personal and into the data, trends, and forces shaping these emergencies. It is only by acknowledging the depth of these issues that we can begin to chart a path toward meaningful change.

It is important to let facts speak to a candid world:

The Mental Health Crisis: How We Got Here and Why It's Worse Than Ever

Mental health struggles have always been part of the human experience, but what are we seeing today? It's on a completely different level.

The scale, intensity, and sheer number of people affected are over-whelming. And it goes way beyond statistics on a page; it's real, and it's unfolding every single day. In classrooms where kids are too anxious to focus. In workplaces where burnout is the norm. In homes where families are barely holding it together. In hospital more and more young people are arriving in crisis.

And if we're being honest? We're not doing nearly enough to stop it.

I've seen it firsthand. I've seen it in my students—the ones who break down because the pressure is too much, the ones who withdraw, the ones who lash out because they don't have the tools to handle what's happening inside them. The ones who are suffering so badly with anxiety that they are incapable of coming to school.

I've seen it in the parents who've lost their children—parents who sit across from me, trying to explain how their bright, promising son or daughter is just *gone*. I've seen it in friends and colleagues who have fought battles no one else could see. And yeah, I've seen it in myself. The weight of it all. The relentless stress, the expectations, the way life just doesn't let up.

So, how did we get here? How did we reach a point where anxiety and depression are the norm, where substance use is skyrocketing, where young people feel like they're drowning, and no one ever taught them how to swim?

The truth is, this crisis didn't appear out of nowhere. It's been building for decades. It's the result of a society that has changed faster than we could keep up with—a world that demands more but gives us less in return. Fewer connections. Less stability. Less time to breathe.

And now, we're here. Facing a crisis that keeps getting worse while the world just keeps moving forward, like nothing is wrong. But some-thing *is* wrong. And until we're willing to face it head-on, nothing will change.

Forgotten America

One of the biggest reasons we're in this mental health crisis is something we don't talk about enough—the way the American economy has completely transformed over the past few decades. People love to say, *Just work hard, and you'll be fine.* But what happens when the jobs that built this country—the ones that gave people a real shot at stability—start disappearing? What happens when an entire way of life gets wiped out, and no one stops to think about what that does to people, to families, to entire communities?

My parents were never shy about teaching us why and how we were so fortunate growing up;

"Nothing good comes easy, you have to work and you have to save."

These words never left my mind. From scraping dirty plates at Schooners and with Marriott Food Services in college, to sweating my ass off in the exterminator trucks while working for my dad. But each of these experiences was spokes in the wheel that brought me all of the spoils I enjoy today.

For many people across America, especially post WWII, manufacturing jobs were all there was, and they would become the backbone of the American economy before globalization really took hold in the 1980s and 90s. Once it did, these jobs were gone, most notably in middle America, where jobs in local industry gave people a sense of community, pride, and purpose.

Growing up in a household where the main income was through small business ownership, we were never hit by the relocation of industry or the shutting down of businesses for employment.

Sure, there were hard times when the economy wasn't strong, but my dad always seemed to recover or have the means to stay afloat when business tanked. But when linking the current mental health crisis to the erosion of economic security in many parts of the country, it's hard to deny the fact that working class communities were hit extremely hard, resulting in many regions being economically gutted, as workers faced a stark new reality of unemployment, job instability, and diminished prospects.

These economic dislocations deeply affected mental health, especially in working-class communities that were ill-equipped to adapt to the rapid shift toward a knowledge-based economy, resulting in rates of substance abuse, depression, and suicide surging in these areas, where economic despair compounded already strained access to mental health care. Many former industrial hubs became towns and cities where unemployment, addiction, and mental illness have become endemic.

Gen Z's "Gig" Economy

Okay, I know I have been adamant about how part-time work for me was a stepping stone, a learning experience, and a stop-gap while I searched for better opportunities. But the truth is, I always understood that these jobs weren't careers. They were part of growing up. The goal was always to move forward, to take what you learned and apply it to something more stable, something that provided benefits, security, and a path forward.

That's not the reality anymore.

Today, with what has become Generation Z's "Gig Economy", a labor market consisting of short-term, flexible jobs instead of traditional full-time employment, jobs that were meant to be part-time are becoming much more than that.

It includes freelance work, independent contracting, and on-demand services like rideshare driving, food delivery, and remote consulting. Platforms like Uber and DoorDash have fueled their growth, offering workers the ability to set their schedules but often without benefits like health insurance, job security, or retirement plans.

I can't tell you how many former students contact me after they've graduated from high school to tell me that they're working in one of these industries. It has become clear to me that my situation, lacking real direction and career paths, mirrors theirs. Years of college followed by no prospects for sustainable careers. Thanks to the concern of Mr. Zocchia and a chance encounter with my parents, I was lucky to stumble upon a teaching position I grew to enjoy.

But many Millennials and Gen Z, who have come of age in this era of economic uncertainty, face an unprecedented combination of student loan debt, high living costs, and unstable job markets. With financial stress as a strong indicator of mental health issues, the strain of insecurity has translated into chronic anxiety and depression for an entire generation of kids who enter the job market after college with limited opportunities. And we need to do better.

Fast Pace America

We're all living it, and it is undeniable. The speed of life in America has never been faster. Every day feels like a race—packed schedule, relentless expectations, and a constant flood of information. We wake up to notifications, rush through our days, and fall asleep with our minds still racing. The demand to always be productive, always be available, and always be striving for more has created a culture where slowing down feels like failure. And in this environment, mental health has taken a major hit.

Somewhere along the way, we lost the ability to cope. Stress, anxiety, and emotional struggles have always been part of life, but past generations had built-in moments to pause, reflect, and reset. Today, those moments are rare. Instead of processing emotions, we distract ourselves—scrolling through our phones, binge-watching shows, or burying ourselves in work. Instead of talking about our struggles, we push through in silence, afraid to appear weak in a culture that glorifies resilience without recognizing that true strength comes from knowing when to ask for help.

I see it every day in the classroom. The pressure on kids is relentless—school, sports, social media, extracurriculars, college applications, all happening at once, with no room to breathe. No time to step back. No space to figure things out. We don't teach kids how to cope with stress in a meaningful way. We don't give them real emotional resilience tools. We don't help them process setbacks or failures. Instead, we push them forward, expecting them to navigate it all without guidance, as if simply moving to the next thing will make the problem disappear.

I had students who turned to substances, not because they wanted to party, but because they needed to escape. I had students who engaged in reckless behavior, not because they were thrill-seekers, but because they didn't know how else to feel something. And I had students who shut down completely, retreating so far inside themselves that they've lost all interest in what's happening around them. I watched kids spiral, and watched the adults around them shake their heads and say, "They just need to toughen up."

The result? A mental health crisis that isn't slowing down. Anxiety and depression rates are skyrocketing. Suicide is one of the leading causes of death for young people. More kids than ever are seeking therapy, but the system is overwhelmed. And instead of addressing the root cause, we've just accepted this way of life as normal, when it's far from it.

Technology's Impact: Connection and Isolation

The rise of digital technology and social media has transformed how people interact and connect. By the early 2000s, the internet had become a dominant force in daily life, and social media platforms such as Facebook, Instagram, and Twitter gained massive popularity. These platforms promised to bring people closer together by creating new ways to communicate, but as social media's influence expanded, it began to change how people perceived themselves and each other.

Not too long ago, I accessed a Facebook page I created in 2008. Compared to what social media is today, it was like traveling through a time warp. Back then, Facebook was novel, but gaining in popularity every single day. It was interesting to see how it had evolved.

Back then, we posted pictures to a "wall" and mused at the comments. We posted brief descriptions of what we were up to that particular day or week, almost an extension of what AOL Instant Messenger was back in the late 1990s. It seemed harmless, and we rarely worried about the ramifications of allowing approved friends into our cyberworlds.

Today, it couldn't be more different. More involved, more intimate, and yes, more daunting, particularly for kids and teens.

Social media today has become a new form of social comparison, where users can curate and broadcast idealized versions of their lives. Adolescents and young adults, in particular, are vulnerable to social comparison, and platforms that reward engagement with likes, comments, and followers have fostered a culture of constant validation-seeking.

Maybe I'm lucky because I see the impact of social media in real time. After all, it is an hour-by-hour staple in the vernacular of teenagers, including my students. In fact, I've gotten pretty good at reading the moods of my students based on what is and is not going on in their social media circles.

It has become their exclusive vehicle of communication, interaction, and comparison.

If something new or exciting happened throughout our lives, we used to come to school the next day with a story to tell, good, bad, or ugly. In today's world, these interactions are spontaneous, fleeting, and just about obsolete by the end of the day. Leaving teens with little time to process, justify, or rectify whatever has happened in their day-to-day lives, and there can be no doubt that it is having a deleterious effect on their mental health.

Studies reveal that high social media use is strongly correlated with increased rates of anxiety, depression, and loneliness, especially among teenagers and young adults. By 2021, the Centers for Disease Control and Prevention (CDC) reported a 40% increase in feelings of hopelessness among teenagers—a spike that researchers attribute, in part, to the pressures of social media.[1]

Cyberbullying has added a darker layer to this dynamic, as online harassment can be anonymous, relentless, and far-reaching. Unlike traditional bullying, which might be limited to specific environments, cyberbullying invades nearly every aspect of a person's life, creating an environment in which victims feel perpetually unsafe. This has led to a tragic rise in depression, self-harm, and suicide among teens. Social media platforms, while designed to foster connection, have inadvertently created spaces where vulnerability is often punished and individuals feel isolated and judged.

Just to piggyback the past with the present, there are ample opportunities for humiliation to play out on social media and reach an audience that far outreaches their present environments. Back in the day, if there was a spontaneous fight between kids, a small circle of people who were in the vicinity witnessed it to tell the tale. Now, videos of fights and the ensuing embarrassment of being on the losing end are recorded and circulated throughout social media in a matter of seconds. Exacerbating the physical scars with emotional ones as well.

Beyond social media, digital dependency has become a widespread issue among adults as well. For those struggling with mental health issues, screens offer a temporary escape. But reliance on digital "numbing" only intensifies feelings of isolation and anxiety, as it prevents people from fully engaging with their own emotions and challenges. The American Psychological Association has highlighted the impact of "doom scrolling"—the compulsion to continuously scroll through negative or distressing news, which became particularly pronounced during the COVID-19 pandemic. This habit can amplify stress and hopelessness, leaving individuals more vulnerable to mental health declines.

And I am guilty of this as charged. The quick scroll from reel to reel on Instagram, or the newest post by a friend on Facebook, or any other social media platform, has completely transformed how we interact with the world, and not for the better.

Barriers to Mental Health Care

The rising need for mental health services has exposed serious deficiencies in the U.S. healthcare system. Mental health services in the U.S. are often prohibitively expensive, fragmented, and poorly integrated into the broader healthcare infrastructure. Many insurance plans offer limited coverage for mental health services, and even with coverage, copays, deductibles, and out-of-pocket costs are significant barriers for many families.

A chronic shortage of mental health professionals exacerbates these issues. According to the Health Resources and Services Administration, over 100 million Americans live in areas with a shortage of mental health providers. This shortage is most pronounced in rural areas, where limited access to mental health professionals forces individuals to travel long distances or rely on primary care providers who may not have specialized training in mental health. This can result in long delays for treatment or no treatment at all.[2]

Additionally, stigma surrounding mental illness discourages many people from seeking help. For years, mental health issues were viewed as personal failings rather than legitimate medical concerns. In certain communities, particularly those with strong cultural expectations of resilience and self-sufficiency, seeking help is often viewed as a weakness. As a result, many people suffering from conditions such as anxiety or depression choose to "tough it out" rather than reach out for support. This quiet suffering is one of the most insidious aspects of the mental health crisis, as it prevents individuals from accessing help until their condition becomes severe.

The Opioid Epidemic: A Public Health Disaster

The opioid epidemic in the 2000s marked a devastating chapter in the mental health crisis. What began as a widespread prescription of opioids for pain relief quickly spiraled into an addiction epidemic, as millions of Americans became dependent on drugs like OxyContin, Vicodin, and later, heroin and fentanyl. Pharmaceutical companies, seeking profit, aggressively marketed these drugs, claiming they were non-addictive and safe for chronic pain management. Doctors, misled by these claims, prescribed opioids at unprecedented rates, and soon, communities across America were awash in addictive painkillers. More on this, later.

Cultural Expectations and the Stigma of Vulnerability

American culture has long celebrated independence, self-reliance, and resilience. While these values have fueled innovation and perseverance, they can also discourage individuals from acknowledging vulnerability. For generations, mental health issues were stigmatized, seen as signs of personal weakness rather than medical conditions requiring treatment. People struggling with anxiety, depression, or trauma were often advised to "tough it out" or "get over it," creating an environment where admitting to mental health struggles was seen as shameful.

This cultural reluctance extends particularly to men, who are often socialized to suppress their emotions and avoid seeking help. Male suicide rates are significantly higher than those of women, especially among middle-aged men, highlighting a hidden crisis among those who feel unable to reach out for support. For many men, the stigma surrounding mental health is a significant barrier, and the pressure to conform to cultural expectations of stoicism only exacerbates feelings of isolation.

For younger generations, cultural stigma has lessened somewhat, thanks to increased mental health awareness and advocacy. However, barriers to seeking help remain. Many view mental health treatment as a last resort, a sign that they are "failing" in some way. Despite increasing awareness, mental health stigma continues to create barriers, leaving many individuals to deal with their symptoms in silence.

The COVID-19 Pandemic: A Surge in Mental Health Issues

In 2020, the COVID-19 pandemic brought new mental health challenges to light. Forced isolation, economic insecurity, and constant uncertainty created an environment in which stress and anxiety could thrive. People across all demographics experienced an unprecedented level of psychological strain, as lockdowns severed social connections, job losses created financial instability, and the threat of illness loomed constantly.

Young people, whose lives were disrupted by school closures, social isolation, and the transition to remote learning, experienced a sharp increase in mental health issues. Studies show that rates of depression, anxiety, and suicidal ideation among teenagers spiked during the pandemic, as many struggled to adapt to an unfamiliar and often lonely way of life. Healthcare workers, on the frontlines of the pandemic, faced extreme levels of burnout, with many experiencing symptoms of PTSD due to the overwhelming demands of their work and the trauma of witnessing widespread illness and death.

The pandemic also exposed deep flaws in America's mental health infrastructure. As demand for mental health services surged, people encountered long wait times, insufficient coverage, and, in some cases, a complete lack of access. Telehealth emerged as a valuable tool, but it was not a perfect solution, as not everyone had access to the technology needed for remote therapy. For many, the pandemic underscored the urgent need for systemic change in how the U.S. approaches mental health care.

Bridging the Personal to the Big Picture

Throughout this journey, I've shared stories, reflections, and personal moments that shaped my understanding of the challenges we face. These experiences—both my own and those of the students I've worked with—provide a window into the human side of a crisis that is often reduced to statistics and headlines. But as important as the personal stories are, they only paint part of the picture.

The broader reality of the mental health crisis is staggering. Behind every story is a system that's failing millions of people, and behind every failure are numbers that are impossible to ignore, representing real lives, real families, and real communities grappling with the weight of a growing epidemic:

The Impact of the Mental Health Crisis in America: A Snapshot

1. Prevalence of Mental Health Issues Across the Population

- Adults: Approximately 1 in 5 adults in the United States— about 50 million people—experience mental illness each year, according to the National Institute of Mental Health (NIMH).[3]

- Severe Mental Illness: Roughly 5% of U.S. adults experience severe mental illness, conditions such as schizophrenia, bipolar disorder, and major depressive episodes that significantly impair daily functioning.[4]

- Increase Over Time: Between 2008 and 2021, anxiety and depression diagnoses doubled among adults, a trend exacerbated by economic insecurity, social isolation, and other stressors. [5]

2. Mental Health Crisis Among Youth and Adolescents

- Anxiety and Depression: According to the Centers for Disease Control and Prevention (CDC), anxiety and depression affect nearly 1 in 3 adolescents. In 2021, more than 44% of U.S. high school students reported persistent feelings of sadness or hopelessness—an increase of nearly 40% from a decade earlier.[6]

- Suicide Rates: Suicide is now the second leading cause of death among individuals aged 10–24. Rates of suicide among adolescents and young adults have increased by over 50% since 2007.[7]

- Emergency Room Visits: There has been a 30% increase in emergency room visits for mental health-related crises among adolescents aged 12–17 over the past decade. Among younger children (aged 5–11), emergency room visits for mental health concerns also spiked by over 25% between 2019 and 2021.[8]

3. Mental Health Crisis Among Children

- Rates of Mental Health Diagnoses: Mental health disorders among children aged 3–17 have been increasing steadily. The CDC reports that around 1 in 6 children in the U.S. has been diagnosed with a mental health condition, such as ADHD, anxiety, or depression. [9]

- Pandemic Impact: The COVID-19 pandemic exacerbated mental health challenges for children, as lockdowns and remote schooling disrupted routines and isolated children from social support. Since 2020, there has been a marked increase in reports of depression, anxiety, and behavioral issues among children.[10]

School Impacts

- School Impacts: Schools report increased mental health-related absenteeism, and educators are observing higher levels of behavioral issues, concentration problems, and social anxiety in students. This disruption affects academic performance and increases the burden on school resources. [11]

4. Socio-Economic Impact

- Economic Cost: The mental health crisis costs the U.S. economy an estimated $200 billion annually due to lost productivity, absenteeism, and disability claims. Depression alone is one of the leading causes of workplace disability.[12]

- Healthcare Strain: Over 100 million Americans live in areas with a shortage of mental health professionals, leading to long wait times and insufficient access to care. The growing demand for mental health services is straining an already overburdened healthcare system, increasing overall healthcare costs. [13]

- Workplace Burnout: Workplace burnout has become a significant problem, particularly in high-stress fields like healthcare, education, and law enforcement. Studies show that nearly 75% of healthcare workers report symptoms of burnout, with many citing mental health as a critical factor. [14]

5. The Role of Social Media and Technology in Youth Mental Health

- Screen Time and Isolation: Studies show that high levels of screen time and social media use are correlated with increased rates of depression and anxiety in teens. Teens who spend more than 3 hours per day on social media are more likely to report mental health issues. [15]

- Cyberbullying: Approximately 15% of high school students report being cyberbullied, and the prevalence of cyberbullying is linked to increased rates of depression, anxiety, and suicidal thoughts among victims. [16]

Social Comparison

- Social Comparison: Social media has been linked to a heightened sense of inadequacy and body image issues among adolescents. Studies reveal that heavy social media use can amplify negative feelings and increase the risk of eating disorders, particularly among teenage girls. [17]

6. Long-term Consequences of Childhood Mental Health Issues

- Academic Impacts: Children with untreated mental health issues are more likely to experience difficulties in school, including lower academic achievement, higher dropout rates, and decreased motivation. [18]

- Future Employment: Mental health issues in adolescence are linked to challenges in adulthood, including higher unemployment rates, difficulty maintaining relationships, and increased likelihood of engaging in substance abuse. [19]

- Cycle of Poverty and Mental Health: Families affected by poverty are more vulnerable to mental health challenges, creating a cycle where mental health struggles hinder economic mobility, while economic stress exacerbates mental health conditions. [20]

The data paints a stark picture: the mental health crisis is pervasive, impacting millions across all age groups and backgrounds, with children and adolescents facing particularly steep challenges. This crisis has profound implications for society, which affect everything from economic productivity to educational attainment and community well-being. Addressing this will require comprehensive solutions spanning healthcare reform, social support systems, educational resources, and technological regulation, especially concerning children and social media use. Only by understanding the full scope of this crisis and its specific impact on the youngest generations can the U.S. begin to implement effective, lasting solutions.

11

THE OPIOID CRISIS:

G rowing up, we were always taught to trust the people around us who were responsible for our health and well-being. Doctors, nurses, Emergency Management workers, Pharmacists, and just about anyone else who presented themselves as trustworthy and responsible.

I remember my pediatrician, Dr. Matthew, an older, balding, and deadly serious Indian American man who was all business. I suffered from seasonal allergies and had to visit Dr. Matthew every week, and truth be told, because of his serious demeanor, he scared the hell out of me as a child. I am 45 years old now, and I honestly believe that if I ever saw Dr. Matthew again, he would still scare the hell out of me as an adult. But you know what? He was my doctor. He gave me allergy shots once a week for 2 years, he prescribed medicine when I was sick, and always made me feel like no matter what, it was his responsibility to make sure I was healthy, no questions asked, and I believed him. Why wouldn't I? His intentions were good, and his remedies were effective.

My mother always felt comfortable with Dr. Matthew's practice, so coming from one trusted adult saying she trusted another, that was enough for me.

I don't know if I feel that way today. From the mid-1980s until present, so much has changed in the medical field that trusting someone you were always taught to trust isn't as black and white as it once was. But I'll come back to this.

I wouldn't be telling the truth if I said that I didn't engage in the typical taboo of late adolescence and early 20s behaviors. More on this later, but I'll provide a glimpse of what that means and why it matters.

Where I grew up, drinking alcohol by the age of 18 was (yes, illegal) but also as socially acceptable as anything else during those formative years, and while I rarely overdid it, casual drinking was just something that we all did at one time or another.

Except by my 19th birthday, sometime in 1999, my second year of college, I noticed something else manifesting in the social circles of high school and college friends. It was pills ,Painkillers, to be more specific.

People were casually finding their way into prescription bottles of legal painkillers and taking them at will.

"It's the best, you drink six beers and take a painkiller, and it's like you drank a twelve pack," I often heard.

"It's not dangerous, they're legal," I also heard.

What did we know? There was no danger on the horizon as far as we knew. If a trusted doctor prescribed these pills, they must be okay. Doctors were our friends. They helped us when we were sick, had allergies, or needed to put a broken bone in a cast. Nothing wrong here, right?

Except there was. By the early 2000s, people around me were taking pills for more than just augmenting a buzz from alcohol. Suddenly, who had a sore back, a migraine, a toothache, or anything that caused even the slightest pain? Pills were everywhere.

They infiltrated our friendly poker games, friends were emptying their parents' medicine cabinets to get their hands on them.

There was a flurry of odd behaviors I couldn't quite wrap my head around, and it always seemed to manifest around the legal, perfectly safe, trusted doctor-prescribed painkiller pills. Nothing to worry about here, I was sure of it.

To be clear, I never fell for it. When I was in my early twenties, I had a sore ankle and was given the only painkiller pill I have ever taken, to this day. Back then, they were in people's pockets like breath mints. I complained of the pain in my ankle, and a friend took out a pill and told me to take it.

"It's okay, my doctor prescribed it to me."

So I took it. Sure, it took the ankle pain away, then proceeded to knock me straight on my ass for what seemed like hours. I was brain dead, nauseous, and looped out of my mind, to the point that I was scared of the lack of control I had over my mind and body. I vomited about five times that day, then never them again.

The moral of this story? I didn't know it at the time, my friends didn't know it at the time, and the general public didn't know it at the time, but by then, the United States was barreling full steam ahead toward the worst drug crisis it has ever seen.

The opioid crisis in America was a story of **corporate greed**, as pharmaceutical companies aggressively marketed addictive painkillers while downplaying their risks. It was a story of **regulatory failure**, where government agencies failed to prevent the overprescription and distribution of opioids despite clear warning signs. It was a story of **medical overreach**, as doctors, under pressure from pharmaceutical representatives and flawed pain management guidelines, prescribed opioids at alarming rates. It was a story of **devastated communities**, where addiction, overdoses, and broken families became widespread, particularly in rural and working-class areas. Finally, it was a story of **delayed accountability**, where lawsuits and public outcry eventually forced some corporate and governmental reforms, but only after count-less lives were lost.

Rewind to the 1990s. Pain management was becoming a major focus in medicine, with doctors rethinking how they treated chronic pain. The goal? Find better ways to help patients without ruining their quality of life.

And then along came Purdue Pharma with a "solution"—OxyContin, a painkiller that was supposedly "safe" because of its time-release formula. Purdue's sales pitch? It works for 12 hours and has almost no risk of addiction. (*Yeah, okay.*)

They spent millions marketing OxyContin as a wonder drug, convincing doctors that opioids weren't just for extreme cases anymore. Suddenly, they were prescribing it for everything—back pain, arthritis, post-surgical discomfort—things that had never required opioids before.

And when some doctors hesitated, Purdue doubled down. They flooded the market with aggressive sales tactics, free samples, and even lavish vacations for doctors who prescribed it.

And guess what? It worked.

By 2001, OxyContin was the best-selling opioid in America, making Purdue billions of dollars while hooking millions of Americans.

Purdue Addicts America

Here's how addiction works:

1 . Doctors prescribe opioids freely, trusting Purdue's "science."

2 . Patients take them as directed.

3. They build up a tolerance and need higher doses to get the same relief.

4. Doctors start to cut them off because—oops—turns out these drugs ARE addictive.

5. Patients, now dependent, turn to heroin and fentanyl to feed their addiction.

This isn't a hypothetical scenario. It happened in real time, to real people, in real towns across America.

Between 1999 and 2011, opioid prescriptions tripled. By 2012, doctors wrote 255 million opioid prescriptions in a single year, which means for every 100 Americans, there were 81 prescriptions floating around.

And it hit some places harder than others.

- Mining and manufacturing towns—places where injuries were common—were flooded with pills.
- Rural areas, where access to alternative treatments was limited, became hotspots for opioid addiction.
- Middle-class suburbs, where people trusted their doctors, saw overdoses skyrocket.

This became so much more than addiction, with entire communities being systematically targeted and impacted.

The Switch to Heroin and Fentanyl: The Crisis Gets Worse

Once people were addicted, the government finally started cracking down on opioid prescriptions. Sounds good, right? Except they forgot one thing—millions of people were already hooked.

So what happens when your legal supply disappears but your body still craves the drug?

You find something else.

And that "something else" was heroin—cheaper, easier to get, and just as effective. By the mid-2010s, heroin overdoses were skyrocketing.

But then things got even worse.

Drug dealers saw an opportunity and introduced fentanyl into the mix —a synthetic opioid 50 to 100 times stronger than morphine. Fentanyl was mixed into heroin, counterfeit pills, marijuana, and cocaine, and users had no idea.

The result? Mass death.

Today, fentanyl is responsible for two-thirds of all opioid-related deaths. One dose. That's all it takes.

The Fallout:

Here's what the opioid crisis has left in its wake:

Drug overdose deaths in the U.S. from 1999 to 2022 exceeded 932,000, with over 700,000 involving opioids specifically.

Billions in profit for the companies that caused it.

Hospitals and rehab centers are overwhelmed with overdose patients.

Hundreds of billions of dollars, including healthcare, lost productivity, and criminal justice costs.

Whole communities are impacted by addiction, unemployment, and crime rates. [1]

And while families were burying their loved ones, the people at the top? They walked away rich. Purdue Pharma finally got sued, but let's be honest—no amount of money brings back the countless lives lost.

The opioid crisis didn't just happen. It wasn't some freak accident or an unavoidable tragedy. It was built, piece by piece, by people who knew exactly what they were doing.

This isn't a story about reckless drug users. This is a story about corporations putting profit over human lives, about a broken healthcare system that allowed it to happen, and about the communities left to clean up the mess.

In just over two decades, opioids have claimed nearly a million lives, leaving behind devastated families, financial ruin, and entire towns in the grips of addiction. And the worst part? The people responsible aren't sitting in prison cells. They're sitting in mansions.

The opioid crisis will go down as one of the most tragic periods in American history. The pharmaceutical companies, responsible for the most effective life-saving drugs on the market, produced legal heroin and marketed it as safe. The doctors we trusted to make us unsick were active assailants in prescribing hundreds of millions of them. All in the spirit of making money, despite who they hurt, or in many cases, killed.

And the government we trusted to oversee the process and prevent maleficence failed us. They are all equal culprits in a vicious cycle that needs vigilance, reform, and accountability.

12

MY UNEXPECTED BATTLE

As mentioned, as a child of the 80's, it was baked in that mental illness was a far-off land, with bridges to cross, with ugly evil trolls living under them, in a dark forest with demons and undertakers and pitchforks, and fires burning. I, along with my entire generation, was ill-prepared for the reality that would manifest

by the second decade of the twenty-first century. By the time I was in my 30s, some semblance of mental illness seemed to be everywhere, closer than I ever imagined.

Summer at my house is always the pinnacle of the year. Ten weeks of vacation, fireworks and fishing and beaching and swimming, and relaxing. When my wife and I first bought our home, we immediately poured whatever money we received from our wedding and what we had in savings into improving the house, specifically so that we could enjoy the summers we both had off from work. New, sprawling decks, an 18x33' swimming pool, hot tub, fire pit, and wide open, beautifully landscaped lawns. We loved to throw parties and spend time with friends and family while we enjoyed summer vacation. Since we were married in 2012, it has become a staple of existence and something we look forward to all year. We would fill the house with kids, family, and friends, and all the trimmings of a settled, quiet, and comfortable life. But like so many unforeseen events, the good life would come with caveats. Caveats that would contribute to a battle I was ill-prepared for, and one that would have profound impacts on life as I knew it.

Adulthood

I guess I could trace the origins back to late 2008, around the time of Barack Obama's historic election. I was 28 and adjusting to the fallout of a broken engagement—a whirlwind of emotions that I can only describe as equal parts relief and uncertainty. It's a long story, but it boils down to this: sometimes, you just have to take out the trash. When the bag is full of debris, you tie it up and take it to the curb.

Without diving into every gritty detail, I made a life-altering decision to call off a doomed marriage just three weeks before the wedding date. Looking back, it remains one of the most courageous things I've ever done. It would've been easier to take the path of least resistance— ignore my instincts, walk down the aisle, and deal with the fallout years later. A messy divorce, lawyers, property disputes, and maybe even children caught in the crossfire. But not me. I was raised to never let a situation spiral so far out of control that it could ruin my life.

So, after three years and a lengthy engagement, I ended it. I was single again at 28. My dad, always ripe with great advice, said it perfectly, "Now don't look back," and that's exactly what I did.

In the immediate aftermath, I felt liberated. Breaking free from the darkness and doom of that relationship was exhilarating. Some choices in life are undeniably right, and when the urgency of making that choice is clear, you don't hesitate. The clarity of the decision gave me an almost euphoric sense of relief.

I used to joke with my friends that it felt like being let out of a cage. The more distance I put between myself and that relationship, the more I realized how much of a bullet I'd dodged. But there's no denying those first few months were difficult. For three years, my identity and daily routines had been entwined with someone else. Pulling the plug on something that significant left an enormous void.

And let me tell you, I didn't fill that void wisely at first. Sure, the newfound freedom was intoxicating, but with endless hours to fill outside of work, I was making choices that were, let's just say, somewhat destructive. I was pushing 30 but behaving like I was 21, and the novelty of that wore off quickly.

I hit a rough patch. It wasn't exactly a midlife crisis—more like a quarter-life reset. But I had no roadmap, no clear direction for what was next. I took the time to embrace being single, and I enjoyed it at every turn. But as I was staring at 30 in the not-too-distant future, with most of my friends married or involved in serious relationships, feeling the void and living alone, I realized I was ready to get back in the game. This time, armed with the knowledge of what I didn't want. Experience is the best teacher, they say.

This was a time before the convenience of dating apps, so meeting someone new wasn't as simple as swiping right. If I were going to find the right person, it would have to happen the old-fashioned way—through chance, mutual friends, or shared environments.

Sure enough, after months of spinning my wheels and rewinding the clock a bit, outside forces intervened. The next chapter of my life I'd been waiting for practically fell into my lap—or, more accurately, into my school.

In early November that year, a new probationary teacher was appointed at our high school. She worked just a few classrooms down the hall from mine, and for a while, I didn't even know she was there. Little did I realize that the person who would change my life forever had already quietly entered the scene.

Melanie

My memory, always sharp and vivid, crackles to life when I think of the first time I met Melanie. It was just a few weeks after she had started her new position at our school. As part of my duties as a special education teacher, I frequently brought tests to the Academic Learning Center (ALC), a designated space where students with accommodations like extended time or tests read would go to take their exams. That day, Melanie was in charge of the ALC, and a seemingly routine stop turned out to be anything but.

Looking back, I'm pretty sure my radar was already firing as I climbed the stairs to the second floor with a test in hand. In the teaching profession, much like with students, news travels fast, especially when it involves a new teacher in the building. Let's call it what it is: gossip. And nothing got the Peanut Gallery buzzing more than the arrival of a new, young, and attractive teacher. By 2008, our school staff was well into a generational turnover, with many of the veteran teachers retiring and being replaced by younger hires. Melanie's arrival had caused a stir, and as I approached the ALC that day, my curiosity was palpable.

What was all the fuss about?

Love at first sight—do I believe in it? Not until that day. Nope, never had. I'd dismissed it as something you only read about in novels or see in the movies. But then I walked into the ALC and BAM. My knees went weak. A rush of heat started at my feet, shot through my entire body, and settled in my face, which I'm certain turned bright red. I could barely get the words out: "I have a tttt-test for…"

Melanie greeted me with a radiant smile, her grace and soft demeanor instantly disarming. As we shook hands, those waves of heat came back, one after another.

"Hi, I'm Melanie. So nice to meet you. I went to school with your sister," she said.

Whoa, a connection! Her calm presence, natural beauty, and the warmth in her voice were almost overwhelming, but the fact that she already had a connection to my family made the moment feel serendipitous. I left the room with my mind spinning, one thought repeating itself: *I'm going to marry that girl.*

I walked back to my classroom, convinced that I had met the woman I was going to marry. After several months of cat and mouse, we were dating.

Melanie and I were fortunate to have a strong foundation from the very beginning. We shared so much in common—our heritage, a deep commitment to family values, a love for education, and a similar vision for the future. We wanted the same things: a family, a stable life close to our parents and siblings, and a partnership rooted in mutual respect and understanding.

What a difference a year makes. People often talk about "just knowing" when they've met the right person. For me, that cliché rang true. It was as if all the doubts, second-guessing, and unease I'd felt in the past had melted away. This time, there was no question: I had gotten it right.

We dated for several years, got engaged, and were married in November 2012. I can still recall the details of our wedding day with perfect clarity. The smell of the catering hall—a mix of fresh flowers and fresh cooking from the kitchen. The scuffed hardwood floors of the reception space. The panoramic views of the Great South Bay through the large windows. The music, the food, the laughter, and the amazing time we shared with 175 of our closest friends and family.

From that moment on, we were off to a fantastic start. Like many young couples at the time, we followed a familiar path. We had stable, well-paying jobs. Housing prices, still low in the wake of the 2008 Great Recession, made it possible for us to buy our first home—a cozy house in Babylon, not far from our families or workplaces.

The honeymoon phase of our marriage unfolded with ease. We were young, in love, and excited to embark on the next chapter of our lives together. But storm clouds were on the horizon. Little did I know, Melanie would become the anchor that would keep me steady through what was to come and the inspiration behind so much of what I've achieved since that fateful day in November 2008.

Our New Home

Owning a home is special—there's no doubt about that. Especially one that fits you and your partner like a glove. During the summer of 2011, the housing market on Long Island was still recovering from the Great

Recession's mortgage crisis. Foreclosures, short sales, zombie houses, and an overwhelming inventory of homes made it a buyer's market, and we were ready to take advantage of it. With money in the bank, steady jobs, and the timing on our side, Melanie and I were ripe to buy our first home.

For those unfamiliar with the south shore of Long Island, particularly Babylon, it's a highly desirable place to settle down and raise a family. Like the community I grew up in, Babylon has great schools, a prime location along the Great South Bay, and a strong sense of community and family values. Typically, houses in Babylon barely hit the market before they're snatched up, often selling through word of mouth. These days, listings in Babylon last an average of 12 days. It's that hot.

But in the summer of 2011, things were different. The market was saturated with homes for sale—big, small, expensive, cheap, move-in ready, and fixer-uppers. For us, it was perfect timing. After a summer of searching, we found the house that checked all our boxes: a spacious four-bedroom Cape Cod on a somewhat busy street but with a yard larger than most in the area. For a couple planning to start a family, it was ideal. Big bedrooms, three bathrooms, a finished basement, and that yard—it practically begged for pickup baseball games with our future kids. It had everything we wanted. By the end of the year, it was ours.

Of course, everything looks shiny on the surface. Our new house was no exception. As two first-time homeowners intoxicated with excitement, we had no idea what was waiting for us. How could we? We'd bought into the "move-in ready" sales pitch, only to walk in on that first day and get slapped with reality.

It quickly became clear that move-in ready for us meant move-out ready for the previous owners.

The rugs in every room were filthy. The walls, riddled with nail holes and scuffs from the previous owner's furniture, needed a fresh coat of paint. The basement, which had seemed so enticing during our walk-throughs, now felt dark, musty, and uninviting. Missing light fixtures, a broken toilet, and a torn, stained runner rug hanging off the staircase

—leftovers from the previous owner's dogs—had us rethinking the lure of "move-in ready".

Sure, it's not unusual for new homeowners to experience this. I'm sure you're thinking, *What did you expect?* And you'd be right. But the truth is, no amount of preparation can fully brace you for the reality of turning a house into your home. Fortunately, we didn't have kids to worry about (yet). We had the financial means and motivation to take on the challenge. So, once the dust settled (and trust me, "dust" is putting it mildly), we got to work.

A good friend once told me, "Owning a home is like setting money on fire." At the time, I thought he was exaggerating. He wasn't.

Movers? Check. Cleaning service? Check. Painters, plumbers, carpenters, and a gas conversion? Check, check, check, and check. Electric bill? Cable bill? Water bill? Check, check, check. A thousand trips to P.C. Richards, Lowe's, Costco, and Bob's Furniture? Oh, and the first mortgage payment?—check.

The first six weeks in our new home were brutal on our wallets. I lost track of how many checks I wrote, but I'm pretty sure it was enough to choke a camel. The costs easily exceeded $10,000—probably closer to $20,000. But we were prepared. Financially stable and motivated, we took the hit to our joint bank account in stride.

We cleaned, painted, replaced, and reimagined the space to reflect our preferences. When we married 11 months later, the house was starting to feel like *our* home. There were still big projects ahead—the basement, the backyard, and the kitchen—but we decided to hold off until after the wedding.

The process of settling into our first home was fun, exciting, exhausting, and expensive. But it was nothing we couldn't handle—at least, not on the surface.

Here's the caveat: before buying the house, we had been living the good life. Two well-paid teachers, one paying minimal rent and the other still living at home, with virtually no financial responsibilities. We ate at nice restaurants, traveled wherever we pleased, and didn't think twice about splurging. We lived on the surface of life, and it was glorious.

Then came the house. And with it, a new reality: bills, repairs, maintenance, and the never-ending expenses that come with homeownership. Even though we could handle it, life as we knew it changed overnight, and the shiny veneer of easy living began to tarnish, just a little bit. Stress counter, #1.

Nicholas

Not surprisingly, Melanie and I settled into our new home nicely. At first, the shock of homeownership—the maintenance, the payments, the unexpected expenses—was overwhelming. But once we established a routine, it became second nature. Before long, our house transformed into a source of pride. Suddenly, raking leaves didn't bother me—it was *my* yard. Shoveling snow? No problem—it was *my* driveway.

We had landed the house we wanted in the community we loved, and we made it truly ours. It was warm, inviting, and perfect for hosting. And we did: parties, BBQs, movie nights, and Sunday dinners. It was a great time to be young, newly married, and surrounded by family and friends.

Eventually, the topic of starting a family crept into our daily conversations. Truthfully, I was terrified. At 32, the idea of parenthood seemed like a distant, abstract concept. Kids were for older, wiser people— parents, not *me*. As Melanie and I soaked up every moment of our first year as a married couple and new homeowners, I thought our carefree life would last forever. But whether through the natural progression of time or some divine nudge, it became clear we were ready to take the next step.

We had stability, a home we loved, and space for pitter-patter. There was nothing holding us back.

I once read that conceiving a child and carrying it to term involve billions of biological processes aligning perfectly. For many, it's a heartbreaking struggle that can take years, if at all. But for Melanie and me, it happened almost immediately—just a month or two after that first conversation. Miracle.

I'll never forget the look on Melanie's face that September morning. Like any new parents-to-be, we started with a trip to the pharmacy for pregnancy tests. Apparently, all those tests—whether the $39 versions at CVS or the 99-cent ones at the dollar store—are equally effective at detecting the hormone that signals conception. Still, wrapped up in the excitement of trying for a baby, I bought five of each, just to be sure.

When the $39 test confirmed what the 99-cent test had shown, Melanie was glowing. Holding up the little stick with the blue plus sign, her voice cracked as she said, "It's positive, honey."

My response? Probably something profound like "Oh my God!" or "Holy shit!"—a mix of disbelief and pure joy. It felt like magic. A few tries, and we were on our way to becoming parents. Nothing could spoil this, right?

Yeah, no.

The initial excitement was palpable. Telling our parents and friends was among the happiest moments of our lives. But lurking beneath the joy was the apprehension, uncertainty, and outright terror of first-time parenthood. For now, though, we took the advice of a friend who'd been through it: "Enjoy the ride."

Well, the ride was bumpy, treacherous, and downright agonizing.

Melanie is a petite woman. She'll kill me for revealing this, but she's maybe 105 lbs, soaking wet. She barely breaks the 5' mark. There is not a lot of room for extra things in her body, let alone a whole new human being. She struggled with the cramped space. She struggled with the discomfort. She was stricken with morning sickness, not for a few months like most other women, but the entire pregnancy. And not morning sickness light.

Not diet morning sickness with a slight twist of lime. Not even morning sickness in the morning, more like all day sickness. All day sickness for 9 months. Vomiting, nausea, headaches, wiped out, knocked on her ass 24/7 all day sickness. I remember her description of it as "the worst hangover you ever had." And for her, it was the length of her entire pregnancy. Ouch.

To Melanie's credit and testament to her strength, she stuck it out. She went to work every day until she literally couldn't walk anymore the final month. She put on a happy face and tried to endure daily tasks and activities to the best of her ability. To this day, I have no idea how she did it. But, she did. By the time May of 2014 rolled around it was time to welcome Nicholas Paul Vecchione into the world. The worst was behind us, so we thought.

The memory is still crystal clear (shocking). Late May on Long Island is a special time of year. I always think of Red from the movie Shawshank Redemption, "May is one hell of a month to be outside". And it is. In the northeast, early spring rains give way to long, balmy afternoons and there are days in May that are longer than days in August. By the last few days of May, especially for teachers, summer, and the relaxing mindset that accompanies it, has just about arrived on Long Island.

So when Melanie woke me up at 1:15 am on May 29th, 2014 saying that her water had broken, the rush out the door and into my Honda Accord was hardly a blur. As we pulled out of the driveway I could hardly contain my excitement. Melanie was almost in full labor, but we both chuckled aloud after I yelled, "Goodbye, house. You will never be the same again!"

I was right. And neither of us knew at that time just how right I was.

After a long, 18 hour labor, Nicholas was born at 6:16pm. He was gray, swollen, full of amniotic fluid and his eyes were glossed over something fierce. But, he was here, and to Melanie and I, he was perfect.

The next two days were what one would expect. A flurry of doctors, nurses, family members, friends, flowers, balloons, pictures, bad hospital meals, sleepless nights, shock, awe, horror, terror, exhilaration , excitement, all of which were stressful, but emphatically overshadowed by the arrival of our first born. By the morning of the third day, it was time to take Nicholas home. He was cleaned up, no longer swollen from 18 hours in the birth canal, and aptly dressed in his new born clothes.

Anyone who has experienced the birth of their first child will agree, those first few days are a vortex of emotions that you can hardly describe. You are elated, relieved, exhausted, wired, hungry, scared and bouncing off just about every wall in your sight, all at the same time. For Melanie and I, it was no different. So when we brought Nicholas home, we put the car seat down in the foyer and stared at him, then at one another, then him, then one another again to a collective "Okay, what do we do now?".

With more visitors, dinners, and introductions in those first few days, the whirlwind would eventually calm down, and our lovely little home was now the home of three. *Gulp.*

While in the hospital, at least back then, they provided the parents with ready-made bottles of baby formula, engineered in some far away laboratory, derived from cow's milk. Whole cow's milk. New parents, like us, don't know any better and begin feeding the baby on some kind of ad hoc schedule. Every two hours, every three hours, then so on. Melanie and I, following protocol, did exactly that and followed suit after we brought Nicholas home. It was whole milk baby formula, every two, three, four hours, on the hour until the baby is in a routine.

To our knowledge, pediatricians tell all new parents not to expect a newborn to follow any schedule for at least a few weeks. It's feed on demand, hope that they sleep, and endure the painful chopped up sleepless nights until the baby is on a feeding and sleeping schedule. Seems simple enough.

Yeah, right!

After a solid three months, no such schedule was ever accomplished with Nicholas. All this baby did was scream, spit up, scream, sleep for 10 minutes, then scream and spit up again. Rinse and repeat for three full months. Luckily, we were out of work for the summer. I say luckily because if either of us had to work during this time, neither of us would have made it. It was a daily dose of hell, and very few professionals had any idea how to help us.

We were new parents, on minimal sleep, trying to nurture a newborn baby who must have been absent the day they taught newborns how to behave,eat, sleep and get into a routine and it was difficult. Very, very difficult.

Finally, after endless visits to the pediatrician, x-rays, sonograms, stool samples (that was fun), and the like, a gastrointestinal doctor concluded that Nicholas was lactose intolerant.

We couldn't believe it. Babies can be lactose intolerant? Who knew? Not us, that's for sure. We had spent three months thinking that this baby was screaming because he was hungry. Because we were told that is what they do when they are hungry. Nicholas screamed so much he must have been hungry, right?

So what did we do? We kept feeding him. Whole milk baby formula. The same whole milk formula the nurses and doctors at the hospital and pediatrician office told us to give him. The same whole milk baby formula that was, unbeknownst to us, tearing his tiny GI tract to shreds. Six, seven times a day. Just bottle after bottle of formula because that's why we thought he was screaming. He would take the entire bottle, sleep for ten minutes, then wake up and spit up and scream again until he was given another bottle. This went on 24 hours a day, seven days a week for three months.

By the time the gastrointestinal doctor figured out that Nicholas was incapable of tolerating the whole milk formula neither one of us could count on both hands the amount of hours of sleep we had gotten since we brought him home that beautiful, balmy, late May morning. I'm probably exaggerating but not by much.

To make matters worse, we had finally gotten answers and the appropriate formula Nicholas could tolerate. But, as promised by his doctor, it would still be a while until his little body healed from the inflammation and acid reflux the whole milk formula had caused. Carnage. Another month of carnage. Another month of no sleep, spit up and screaming. It would be the middle of September, and we were back to work before we finally got Nicholas scheduled and on a routine.

New parents are up against it. A lot is trial and error and eventually everyone settles in and by month two the baby is somewhat scheduled and on a routine. Melanie and I didn't have that luxury. Augmenting this stress was the lack of sleep and lack of answers to help our obviously suffering baby for the better part of four months. It was the hardest four months of my life. So I thought. *Stress counter #2*

Matthew

Settling into parenthood with Nicholas was no easy feat. Those first four months were an unrelenting onslaught—day after day, night after night, we were battered by exhaustion, frustration, worry, and confusion. Adding to the whirlwind was the discovery that Nicholas had torticollis, a condition that caused his head and neck to tilt abnormally due to cramping in the womb. His case was severe, exacerbating the acid reflux already wreaking havoc on his tiny body. Weekly trips to a physical therapist became part of our routine, along with daily home exercises designed to stretch his neck and shoulders.

Those stretches were nothing short of excruciating—for him and for us. The sound of his screams during each session is forever etched in my memory. It was agony to watch, and yet, we persevered. For nearly a year, this was our life. By the time Nicholas was able to sit upright without assistance, it felt like we had climbed a mountain. Looking back, I often ask myself how Melanie and I managed to survive it all— how we kept Nicholas alive and thriving despite everything. It felt like a miracle, but we did it.

As challenging as it was, there were moments of pure joy nestled between the chaos. Nicholas had an incredible sense of humor for such a tiny human. He was playful, mischievous, and always quick with a bashful grin that could melt your heart. Watching him grow, celebrating each new milestone, and seeing the bond between him and Melanie deepened my love for them both in ways I never thought possible.

Despite the stress of Nicholas's ailments, sleepless nights, demanding teaching jobs, and our hectic schedules filled with doctors' appointments and late-night pharmacy runs, we found a rhythm. By the time the calendar turned to the new year, we were settled, content, and adjusting to our new normal. What could possibly disrupt this newfound harmony, right? *Gulp.*

It was mid-March 2015. Nicholas was walking, sort of talking, and filling our home with laughter. For me, March always brings a boost in mood—winter is finally on its way out, and the promise of summer is on the horizon. Baseball, beach days, and sunshine were en route. But one cold, dreary evening, as I walked into the house after finishing my second job, I was greeted not by warmth and laughter but by silence. An oddity considering the tumult of the previous 10 months.

The house was dark, except for the light coming from the upstairs bathroom.

"Mel, I'm home," I called out.

No answer.

"Mel?"

Still no answer.

Finally, Melanie emerged from the bathroom, pale and holding a thermometer.

"It says I don't have a fever, but I feel like crap," she said, her voice hoarse and cracking.

"What's wrong?"

"I don't know. I have a headache, I'm nauseous, and I feel weak."

"Did you take Advil?"

"Yes, but it's not working," she replied.

What I said next was meant as a joke—a ridiculous, off-the-cuff comment that even surprised me as the words left my mouth.

"Maybe you're pregnant," I said with a laugh.

"Ha, yeah right. Imagine?" Melanie chuckled weakly.

"I mean, this is exactly how you felt when we found out you were pregnant with Nicholas."

"Don't be crazy. It's impossible," she said firmly.

"It's not *that* impossible," I teased, adding a wink for good measure.

"Paul, there is no way. Don't even joke about that," she shot back.

"Okay, humor me. There should be a test or two left in the drawer from last time."

"You're crazy, but fine—just to prove you wrong."

Yeah, there was no wrong to be proven.

The second red bar on the test blared across the testing window almost immediately. Melanie, for the second time in 18 months, was pregnant.

"OH MY GOD!" Melanie yelled. Tears streamed down her face as she repeated it over and over. "OH MY GOD! OH MY GOD!"

The shock hit her like a freight train. She was sobbing, wailing, overcome with panic. Memories of her difficult pregnancy with Nicholas, the sleepless nights, the constant worry, and the chaos of those first months came flooding back. We had just calmed the waters with the shock that came with Nicholas. *Gulp!*

I tried to comfort her, though I was still processing the news myself. Melanie quickly ran back into the bathroom to vomit. Maybe from the baby sickness, maybe from the sheer terror of the news. But, either way I eventually meandered down the steps and found myself downstairs, beer in hand, dialing my brother Bobby. I needed someone to tell, someone to help me process what felt like an awesome but terrifying surprise.

This pregnancy was unplanned, but we would eventually come to terms with it and treat it as it was— a blessing. Once the initial shock wore off, we sprang into action—prenatal vitamins, doctor appointments, and all the steps to ensure Melanie's health and the baby's. But as the weeks passed, the excitement was tempered by a series of setbacks.

At her three-month checkup, the doctors struggled to locate a heartbeat. An ultrasound revealed an embryo, but no sound of life. It was a bleak start and we were devastated. Blood tests confirmed Melanie was indeed pregnant, but the uncertainty lingered. Finally, a month later, we heard the tiny, miraculous sound of a heartbeat. Relief washed over us—but not for long.

Melanie's second pregnancy was even harder than her first. The morning sickness returned with a vengeance—24/7 for six months. On top of that, every doctor's visit seemed to bring new concerns: slow growth, low amniotic fluid levels, and troubling scans that hinted at potential birth defects. By the time her due date approached, the doctors had painted a grim picture of what we could expect. It wasn't good but we held out hope that the baby would arrive healthy, and abortion was never an option.

On November 3, 2015, Melanie went into labor. It was quick—just 45 minutes, with no time for an epidural. At 10:22 p.m., Matthew John Vecchione entered the world.

They whisked him away immediately. For what felt like an eternity, Melanie and I sat in silence, holding our breath, trying not to focus on the flurry of bad news and possible bad outcomes we had been warned about throughout the duration of her pregnancy.

Finally, the nurse returned with our son.

Matthew was perfect. Seven pounds, eleven ounces of bright dark pink, healthy, vibrant baby boy. The thick head of hair that crowned him looked like a tiny helmet. All of the uncertainty, fear and unease evaporated in an instant. Modern medical science is nothing short of remarkable, but they had gotten this one completely wrong, and we couldn't have been happier.

Our gratitude and exhilaration got us through the next few days. Melanie stayed with Matthew in the hospital while I was home taking care of Nicholas. By day three, it was time to take Matthew home. *Gulp*.

If, when we brought Nicholas home we had to look at each other and ask "what do we do now?", no such question had to be asked when we walked through the door with Matthew. We knew what to do. But now we had to do it with a 16 month old tearing up the house. That first night was challenging. Very challenging. And, a prelude of what was to come.

By the time we had reached mid winter, our new reality was in full swing. Two babies, one in full destructive mode and one in full infant mode. Except, as the script unfolded, it was one we had seen before. Torticollis, formula intolerance, acid reflux, untenable lack of sleeping routine and bout after bout of colds, ear infections, and vomiting. In his first year of life, Matthew was infinitely more difficult than Nicholas ever was. Added to that were the trips to the pediatrician, the late night pharmacy runs, the physical therapist, the gastrointestinal specialists and the ENT doctor, this time, times two. All of this, piled onto the difficult scenarios we were enduring with Nicholas, and now having to tend to Nicholas as we took care of Matthew made the first year of child number two an epic saga for the books. Except it wasn't in the books, it was our day to day lives. In what seemed like an instant, the days of fancy restaurants, BBQ's and fun with family and friends had evaporated. Two incredibly difficult babies in 2 years. *Stress counter #3.*

Two Jobs

Remember when I said I never wanted to be a teacher? And remember those early anecdotes of my teaching career, the struggles, the challenges, and the endless tribulations? Yeah, they were real. They were perpetual during the first decade of my career, shaping my experience as a young educator. But, as difficult as they were, they also served as life lessons, teaching me how to adapt, endure, and improve.

Full disclosure: I wouldn't call my craft of teaching "perfect," far from it, even now, but by the time I entered my second decade as an educator, I had developed the skills to confidently say I was good at it. I had mastered classroom management and forged meaningful relationships with my students, a skill that, for me, has always been the cornerstone of effective teaching.

Looking back at my very first interview in 2005, I can't help but cringe. I was nervous, eager, and convinced I had all the right answers. Sitting across from a panel of seasoned educators, I proudly detailed my qualifications: two master's degrees, a knack for working with kids, experience writing for my college newspaper, punctuality, responsibility, and being a good role model for teens, blah blah!.

Yeah, no.

That table full of administrators probably chuckled to themselves as I recited my résumé like a grocery list. What I didn't realize back then, but now know to be the essence of great teaching, is that the foundation of success in the classroom isn't rooted in college degrees or college journalism—it's in the ability to build trust and relationships with students.

Kids are sharp. They can spot insincerity a mile away. They know when you're being real with them and when you're full of shit. I've always been real with my students, and I think that's why I've been able to reach them. Yes, I'm the authority figure in the room, equipped with degrees and knowledge they need to succeed. But they also know we're on the same team. I'm their coach, and they're my teammates, working together to meet a common goal.

If only I'd known this during that first interview. But, as they say, experience is the best teacher.

By the time I hit my 10-year teaching mark, I decided to expand my day and start teaching English at the alternative school in my district. It was a natural fit—by then, I had experience with both content and at-risk students. The opportunity to reach even more kids was inviting, and the extra money didn't hurt, especially with two boys in diapers and the endless pile of house bills to pay.

In 2015, the year Matthew was born, I was well into teaching two English classes at the alternative school, twice a week. The hours weren't ideal—5:00 to 6:15, then 6:40 to 7:55—but the financial boost made it tolerable.

Before kids, this arrangement was manageable. Melanie appreciated the quiet evenings to herself, and I was content with the extra cash the second job brought in and it funded our endless home improvement projects. Life was busy, but it worked.

Then the boys arrived.

Working nights while raising two incredibly challenging boys under the age of two was a whole different ball game. Nicholas was barely a toddler, and Matthew was an infant, each with health complications. The chaos at home—screaming, sleepless nights, constant doctor visits —was relentless. Adding a second job to the mix stretched us to our limits.

A sense of guilt hit me every time I walked out the door at 5 p.m. Melanie, already exhausted, would be wrestling to take care of Matthew, who was screaming at the top of his lungs, while Nicholas wreaked havoc in the living room—throwing toys, food, and anything else he could get his hands on.

On the drive back to school, already working on minimal sleep, I'd struggle to keep my eyes open, knowing I had three hours of teaching ahead of me, after the six hours at my day job. The students in my night classes were at risk and often difficult to manage, requiring every ounce of patience and energy I had left. By the time I got home, the chaos was still waiting for me: a whirlwind of toys, vomit, fevers, and toddlers who refused to sleep.

It's no wonder those years are such a blur. To this day, I'm not entirely sure how we survived them. Juggling two jobs and two babies was one of the most challenging periods of my life. But somehow, we made it through.

Not without a cost, though. Stress counter: #4.

Home Improvement

No, not the Tim Allen sitcom from the 1990s. While *Home Improvement* was funny and entertaining, it gave a wildly misleading impression of what the reality of improving your home is actually like. The humor, the quick resolutions, the quirky projects—it all painted a picture that home improvement was not only manageable but enjoyable. Spoiler alert: it's not.

The truth about home improvement is simple: it sucks.

When Melanie and I first bought our home, I told you how intoxicating and exciting the process was. We had found a great house in the community we loved and it felt like the embodiment of the American Dream—a young couple poised to build a future, complete with a white picket fence and all the trimmings. We were convinced the house was "move-in ready."

Ah, youth and naivety.

Move-in ready meant the walls were standing, the appliances were turned on, and the lights worked. But once the previous owners were gone, we realized they had dressed the house up just enough to sell it. Beneath the surface, it was a different story. From dusty, musty carpets to scratched floors, nail holes in the walls, and a basement that reeked of dampness, it became abundantly clear that this "move-in ready" house was anything but ready for us.

Still, we got it into livable shape during that first year. It was hard work but rewarding. And then, as new homeowners often do, we realized that "livable" wasn't enough. The house needed upgrades—serious ones.

The first thing on my dream list? A pool. I had grown up with a pool, and because I barely used it, in my new home, I always wanted a pool, so that first winter, we went shopping and found the biggest one on the market—a monstrous 18'x33' semi-inground. By spring, they broke ground, and before we knew it, the pool was in. **Check.**

Next was the basement. It was massive, spanning the entire house, but it was a disaster. Dust, must, and a layout that needed a complete overhaul. Melanie's uncle, who owned a construction company, swooped in, and by summer, our mornings were soundtracked by the sweet symphony of drills, nails, and drywall. A few walls came down, a bathroom and laundry room went up, and with some fresh carpet and paint, the basement became an excellent addition to our home. **Check.**

Of course, what's a big pool without a big deck? Around the pool it went, wrapping around the hot tub and extending into the yard. **Check.**

And because we weren't finished spending money, we added a new deck off the back of the house with an overhang, complete with ceiling fans to boot. **Check.**

By the time we celebrated our first wedding anniversary, we had transformed our new house into our home. It was spacious, inviting, and perfect for hosting our large families and groups of friends. We were living the dream.

But, as I've mentioned, life has a way of throwing curveballs.

Within 17 months, Nicholas and Matthew had made their grand entrances, and our once-spacious home felt like it was shrinking daily. Parents know what I'm talking about—kids come with an avalanche of *stuff*. Toys, clothes, baby gear, and all the chaos they bring. Our home went from feeling open and airy to a cluttered labyrinth of high chairs, diaper bags, baby swings, toy chests and an endless stream of laundry.

By the time Matthew's third birthday rolled around, Melanie and I were faced with a tough choice: move or renovate. Neither of us wanted to leave the home we had poured so much into, so we decided it was time for a major renovation.

The plan was ambitious: combine two small bedrooms to create a master suite with a bathroom, gut the kitchen and modernize it, and convert the garage into a family room. After months of deliberating, we finally found a contractor in late 2018 who came highly recommended and had a practical, affordable plan. His timeline? Two months. His promise? Daily work, minimal disruption, and high-quality results.

Yeah, no.

As they say, "We make plans, and God laughs." This renovation quickly devolved into a nightmare. Our contractor turned out to be a full-time county employee, which meant he could only work on our house in the late afternoons and weekends—something he conveniently forgot to mention before we signed the contract.

The first project—the master suite—was riddled with cut corners and shoddy decisions. Sure, the result was fine, but it wasn't what we had envisioned. And then came the kicker: he demanded an additional 25% over the budget due to "unforeseen costs." Against my better judgment, I paid it.

Ever realize just how dependent you actually are on a fully functioning kitchen? We never did, until it was time to renovate ours. And, true to form, the contractor did us no favors in making it more tolerable.

He gutted the entire kitchen, down to the studs, then disappeared for 2 weeks. Unreachable.

Remember that we had two small children to take care of, feed, and cook for, and send to school with lunches for, and whose food and beverages we had to keep refrigerated. He didn't seem to care. He left the kitchen completely stripped to the bones, with nothing but a functioning microwave to use. It was awful, and it became obvious that it was par for the course with this guy.

He was so disorganized and ad hoc that it would be a full 7 weeks before our kitchen was usable again. Plumbers, electricians, missed appointments, sad stories, bullshitting and starts and stops, brought us to the end of May, when the entire renovation was supposed to be done. Nope, only ⅔ was done at this point. And, wouldn't you know it, he went over budget again. Oh, the silliness.

You guessed it, about 25% over budget to be exact. It was as if he had that number in his mind the entire time.

But, like before, I knew that we needed him to finish the job in its entirety. We still needed to convert the garage. So, like before, I reluctantly negotiated the 25% down to a number I could live with. I won't say I was happy about it, or even cooperative about it. I was beyond pissed off.

By the time we got to the garage conversion, I was at my wits' end. I negotiated like hell and kept a closer eye on the work. To his credit, this phase went smoother, likely because he wanted to be done with me as much as I wanted to be done with him.

When the dust finally settled—literally—our home was everything we had hoped for. The renovation gave us the space we desperately needed, but it came at a cost: five months of disarray, more sleepless nights, and unrelenting stress.

The experience taught me valuable lessons about patience, perseverance, and the importance of choosing the right contractor. But let me be clear: home improvement is not for the faint of heart. Even under the best circumstances, it's grueling. For us, with two young kids and an unreliable contractor, it was nothing short of hell. Stress counter: #5.

13

HEAD ON FIRE

As I begin this next chapter, I want to acknowledge what might be running through your mind after reading the previous sections of this story: *Cry me a river! Poor you!* And, honestly, you'd have a point.

Who, in their right mind, would have the audacity to chronicle moments of their life that include marriage, parenthood, a steady job, a second well-paying gig, and the means to renovate a home in a desirable community—all while making it sound like they were *complaining*?

"First World Problems," you might say. And you'd be right. But here's the thing—they were *my* "First World Problems." And there's something significant about that, which I hope to clarify as we move forward.

When I talk to friends and family about my life, I do so with the utmost understanding of how blessed I am. I often say, *"I'm better off than 90% of people in the world."* In a world of nearly eight billion, that's no small thing. I'm fully aware of this privilege, and I cherish it. Every. Single. Day.

I narrowly escaped what would have been a disastrous marriage, calling off my engagement just weeks before the wedding. That decision, as gut-wrenching as it was, became one of the most courageous choices I've ever made. Most people in my shoes might have just gone through with it, hoping for the best and dealing with the fallout later. But I saw the warning signs and had the clarity to act on them when it mattered most. **Gratitude.**

By my 29th birthday, I had met Melanie, the person I was meant to be with. A twist of fate, a chance phone call, and a last-minute job offer brought her to my school that November day in 2008. If not for that phone call, she would have started working in another district, and our paths might never have crossed. **Gratitude.**

By 2011, as the country struggled through the aftermath of the Great Recession, millions of Americans were out of work, losing their homes, and battling despair. Yet, Melanie and I were planning a fairytale wedding and driving around Long Island shopping for a house we could afford in an amazing community. **Gratitude.**

We conceived two beautiful, healthy boys in just over a year—an experience so many couples can only dream of. When so many endure heartbreak, years of trying, and thousands of dollars spent on fertility treatments, Melanie and I were blessed with not just one but two miracles. **Gratitude.**

Today, as the wealth gap widens and housing becomes unattainable for so many, we've not only been able to afford and renovate our home, but we've also had the opportunity to take on extra work to support our family. **Gratitude.**

So, let me be clear: I'm not *complaining*. Not for a second. I'm blessed beyond measure, and I know it. But the story I'm telling isn't about complaints. It's about context. It's about how even a life filled with blessings can reach a breaking point when all the stressors converge at once.

I'm setting the scene for what would ultimately become the most difficult battle of my life—an unexpected fight that was years in the making, forged by the very blessings I just described.

Perspective

To frame the next chapter of this story, I need to provide some additional background. I grew up in what most would consider an idyllic environment: a loving, supportive family in a stable suburban community. Big house, siblings, extended family, vacations, and all the opportunities a kid could want. My parents were happily married, and my upbringing was solid. Sure, there were bumps along the way—painful breakups in high school and college, sibling squabbles, and the inevitable sting of loss as relatives passed—but overall, my life was void of serious adversity.

Even when I struggled to find my footing before becoming a teacher, I still never felt like life was *hard*. I didn't know what it meant to endure true hardship. And as strange as it sounds, that lack of adversity left me ill-prepared for what was to come.

When you've spent nearly three decades living a life of smooth sailing, you don't have the tools to navigate storms, especially when those storms hit all at once.

The Breaking Point

Between 2012 and 2016, my life changed drastically. I was married, a homeowner, and a father to two incredibly challenging boys born just 16 months apart. I was juggling two demanding jobs, managing home renovations, paying bills, setting up college funds, and constantly worrying about my kids' health. Each day was a relentless grind. Each night brought more stress.

For the first time in my life, I felt truly overwhelmed. There was no escape, no reprieve. Every aspect of my life felt *hard*—harder than anything I had ever experienced.

Sleep? Forget it. Any medical professional will tell you that quality sleep is among the most important elements of wellness. Being deprived of sleep is how they break down even the most hardened criminals and international terrorists. And I was deprived of sleep for over four years.

The pit in my stomach was constant. My mind raced with what felt like a thousand fires burning all at once. It was stress on a level I didn't know how to process. My head felt like it was *on fire.*

Years later, I would come to understand that this was a pivotal moment in my life—a moment that forced me to face challenges I had never imagined and would ultimately reshape my perspective. None of the stress factors were novel to most people, but they were new to me in a short period, and at the time, all I could feel was the heat.

The Drive

The human brain is fascinating—an enigma wrapped in complexity. It's humanity's first supercomputer, capable of incredible feats, and I'll borrow a line from Red from the movie *The Shawshank Redemption,* "a complete fucking mystery."

Despite remarkable advances in psychology, even the experts are still often in the dark when it comes to fully understanding the inner workings of the human mind. So when I was first told I was suffering from anxiety, my immediate reaction was disbelief.

"Huh?"

It didn't make sense to me. Anxiety? That was for other people—not for someone like me who always had their shit together. But I wasn't going to argue. Something was undeniably off, and whether or not I wanted to believe it, I had to confront it. It would take a physical manifestation to truly make me a believer. And this came about during a routine drive down the Southern State Parkway.

For a 17-year-old still in high school, having an early birthday doesn't mean much, except when it's time to get your driver's license. Back then in New York, you could get a conditional license at 16 and, with Driver's Education and the 5-hour course, a full license with no restrictions at 17. Thanks to my January birthday, I was the first in my friend group to reach this milestone.

Having a full license at 17 meant one thing: **freedom.**

When I finally passed my road test (on the second try), my dad handed me the keys to a used 1985 Toyota Camry. That car might as well have been a Lamborghini in my eyes. It was my ticket to independence, and I treated it like gold.

It was always clean—so clean that I made my friends knock the dirt off their shoes before getting in. I kept a full tank of gas, cash in the glove compartment for emergencies, and sunglasses in the console for sunny days. Driving around town as a young teen with my friends in the car was the coolest thing at the time.

I spent my late teens and twenties cruising the highways of Long Island and beyond. The Southern State Parkway was one of my most frequented routes—a stretch of road connecting Nassau and Suffolk counties with twists, turns, and tight exit ramps. I must've driven it hundreds of times without a second thought. It was familiar, almost routine. Until it wasn't.

By my mid-thirties, with the aforementioned storms raging around me, things began to change.

It was late August, a warm and humid evening. Our contractor was wrapping up renovations at the house, and my older brother, Bobby, had invited the family out to dinner at a restaurant in Nassau County. Naturally, the fastest way to get there was the Southern State Parkway.

We loaded the boys into their car seats, and Melanie sat with them in the backseat, allowing my dad, who had come along for the ride, to sit shotgun. Just a quick 25–30 minute drive, depending on traffic. What could go wrong?

About five minutes into the drive, the warning signs began.

First, my heart started pounding. *Ba-boom. Ba-boom. Ba-boom.*

Then came the heavy breathing. *Hhhh... Hhhh...*

Heat spread through my body like wildfire. I yanked off my hat and sunglasses, trying to cool down.

Next, the tremors set in—uncontrollable shaking from the waist up.

Finally, the worst of all: my vision narrowed into a terrifying tunnel, leaving me with no peripheral sight and a suffocating feeling of claustrophobia.

It was a full-blown panic attack. And I was behind the wheel, going highway speed, with my entire family in the car.

The Southern State, a road I'd driven countless times, suddenly felt like an unrelenting death trap. At one point, my hands were shaking so badly that my dad had to grab the steering wheel to keep us from careening into the trees lining the road.

I pulled over as soon as I could. My dad took the wheel and drove us the rest of the way.

That drive was a wake-up call.

I'd had panic attacks before, but never this bad. And never with such high stakes. My wife, my children, my father—all of them could've been seriously hurt or worse. The realization hit me like a brick wall: *This can't continue. It just can't.*

I'm a husband and a father. I have responsibilities. I couldn't allow something as simple as driving to dinner to become a life-threatening ordeal.

Later that night, I sat alone in the backyard, rocking in a chair as the sun set. The cool evening air offered some peace, but my mind was racing. I needed a solution, and fast.

Melanie came out to join me. She always knew when I needed her, and her concern for others is one of her most profound qualities. We talked for over an hour, agreeing that something had to change.

"You can't live like this," she said. "We've gotta do something."

"I'll figure it out. Don't worry," I replied.

But there was no "figuring it out." I was lost, consumed by my thoughts and incapable of finding a way forward.

The episodes continued. Until one day, Melanie took matters into her own hands.

"I found you a therapist," she said. "He's right here in town, and I made an appointment for you."

I wasn't happy.

The ancient stigma surrounding mental health was still fresh in my mind. A therapist? Seriously? Therapists were for *other* people—people with trauma, addiction, or severe mental illness. Not for me. I wasn't crazy. I was just... stressed.

"I'm not going," I told her.

Melanie didn't push. She never does. She knows that when she plants a seed, I'll eventually come to the right decision on my own.

Deep down, I knew she was right. But admitting it—and taking that first step—was a battle all on its own, the manifestation of the conditional stigma that surrounded mental health my entire life.

A Walk Around the Pool Deck

The day of the appointment was here—10:30 AM, just two miles from my house, but I still had no intention of going.

In the rhythms of the school year, it was structure, planned schedules, and predictable routines. But summer was different. Summers were for breaking the mold, for taking life one unscheduled day at a time.

Still, a few small routines lingered, and one of them was cleaning the pool.

The pool, that enormous, semi-inground monstrosity we installed during our first year in the house, was a great addition to our yard, but it needed constant upkeep, thanks to the century-old oak trees that loomed over the backyard, sprinkling their leaves and debris into the water like confetti at a never-ending party. I didn't mind, though. It got me outside and kept me busy. Three times a week, I'd skim and vacuum the pool. It was a moment of peace, standing in the sunshine, listening to the morning birdsong, and feeling a quiet satisfaction in doing something productive.

But not that morning.

The night before, sleep had eluded me. I was still wrestling with the storm raging in my mind. The shame of the Southern State Parkway incident loomed large. The indecision about seeing a therapist was gnawing at me. The stigma of it—*a shrink? For me?*—clawed at my pride.

"I don't need help," I kept telling myself. "I can handle this on my own. I always have."

But as I stepped out onto the pool deck that morning, skimmer in hand, I felt the storm brewing.

At first, it was subtle—a shift in the atmosphere, like the moment before a thunderclap. Then it hit.

Ba-boom. Ba-boom.

My heart began to race. The tightening in my chest came next, wrapping itself around my ribcage like a vice. My vision blurred, and I felt the heat rise in waves, like a fire burning just beneath my skin.

Everything near my body felt oppressive: the weight of my shirt, the sunglasses perched on my nose. I tore them off, desperate for relief. But it didn't come.

Instead, I found myself gripping the railing of the pool deck, struggling to catch my breath, fighting to calm the chaos inside me.

This wasn't the Southern State Parkway. There was no speeding traffic, no family in the car depending on me, no life-or-death stakes. This was my backyard. My safe haven. The sun was shining. The birds were singing. And yet, here I was, being consumed by a full-blown anxiety attack.

It didn't make sense. *Why now? Why here?*

Anxiety is an enigma. It doesn't play by any rules. It doesn't announce its arrival or explain its reasons. It crashes in like a rogue wave, leaving you gasping and flailing for air. It's the body's natural state of protection mode when danger is present. But this day, there was no danger present. I was in my backyard skimming my pool. It made very little sense.

Looking back, I could rationalize the panic on the highway. Maybe, in some twisted way, my brain was trying to protect me, trying to keep my family safe by putting my body into overdrive. It wasn't logical, but at least it was *something*.

That's when it hit me.

"You've got a problem, and you need to take care of it."

The realization wasn't gentle. It wasn't some quiet epiphany, sneaking in through the back door of my mind. It was a slap across the face, a gut-punch that left no room for denial.

I put down the skimmer, walked off the pool deck, and went straight into the kitchen, where Melanie was making breakfast for the boys.

She looked up from the stove, her expression immediately shifting from curiosity to concern.

"What's wrong?"

I took a deep breath, still shaky, and finally let the words tumble out.

"Okay. I'll go."

She paused for a moment, as if to let the words settle. Then she gave me a small, relieved smile.

"Good."

There wasn't a hint of "I told you so" in her voice—just quiet encouragement, the kind she had been offering me all along.

In that moment, I felt a strange mix of emotions. Relief, for finally letting go of the fight I'd been waging against myself. Embarrassment, for not admitting sooner that I needed help. Gratitude, for Melanie's patience and quiet persistence.

The truth was, I was scared. Scared of what the therapist might uncover. Scared of what it would mean to admit that I wasn't invincible. But in that moment, as I stood in the kitchen, looking at my wife and my kids, I knew I had to face it. Not just for me, but for them.

The battle within me had reached its peak. And finally, I had chosen the right path.

Melanie knew I would all along. Genius.

14

MY BATTLE WITH ADDICTION

Okay, truthfully, "battle" isn't the word I should use to describe my experience with addiction. More like brush up. For many, it's an all-out war, but for me, it was something different—less overtly destructive, and less consuming. While I've avoided traditional addictions like alcohol or illicit drugs, I haven't been immune to the lure of dependence. And there is one psychoactive substance, nicotine in particular, that has been around much of my life.

Nicotine

My first cigarette wasn't some rebellious teenage act; it happened when I was in fourth grade. Yes, you read that right—fourth grade! I was nine years old, still a child. I didn't know how to inhale, and I doubt I even enjoyed it. But that didn't matter. Smoking that cigarette was all about curiosity(go figure), emulating the adults around me, and stepping into a world I barely understood. When my parents found out, their reaction was as swift as it was harsh. I promised them I'd never smoke again, and for a few years, I kept that promise. But by middle school, the cigarettes found their way back into my hands, and this time, they stayed.

Back then, in the early 1990s, smoking wasn't the cultural taboo it is today. Cigarette ads were everywhere—on TV, in magazines, on billboards, even at Yankee Stadium. Joe Camel grinned at us from every convenience store window, and Marlboro encouraged us to collect "Miles" to redeem for jackets, camping gear, and pocket knives. Smoking back then was normalized, glamorized and omnipresent.. Movie stars, musicians, and even school nurses smoked. For kids like me, cigarettes seemed like the ultimate accessory—dangerous, rebellious, and effortlessly cool.

Peer pressure played its part too. Most of my friends smoked, and in our world, it was practically a rite of passage. A friend showing up to a pickup basketball game with a pack of cigarettes he stole from an unsuspecting grandparent was cause for excitement. We smoked on the sly, thrilled by the act of defiance. By the time I reached high school, smoking was a full-fledged addiction.

The irony, of course, was that we knew better. The dangers of smoking had been public knowledge for decades. But at 14, 15, or 16, we felt invincible. Heart disease, lung cancer, addiction—those were problems for older adults. or for future us who would eventually see the error of our ways, not the kids puffing away behind the bleachers.

Looking back, it's clear that my addiction was born from a perfect storm of influences: accessibility, glamorized advertising, peer pressure, and even the example set by my parents. It wasn't until my 30th birthday—and countless failed attempts—that I finally quit smoking for good.

But while I managed to kick cigarettes, I've never fully escaped nicotine. Even now, at 45, I'm still addicted. Nicotine looms in the background of my daily life, as persistent as ever. I've traded cigarettes for "safer" alternatives: gums, patches, pouches, and the occasional cigar. These substitutes may spare my lungs, but they haven't silenced the cravings. The psychological pull of cigarettes remains strong, a nagging whisper in the back of my mind that never truly fades.

I don't miss the hacking cough, the sore throats, or the lingering stench of cigarettes. I don't miss the way they ruled my life. But I'd be lying if I said I don't still think about smoking. Quitting cigarettes improved my health immeasurably, and for that, I'm grateful. Yet nicotine's hold on me remains, a reminder of how insidious addiction can be.

Breaking free of cigarettes was one of the hardest things I've ever done. But even as a "non-smoker," I carry the weight of addiction. It's a battle I fight daily—a battle I may never fully win.

Gambling

The casino marketing geniuses and PSA commercials on TV seem to think they have the appropriate tag line for pulling the one armed bandit, rolling the bones, going all in: "When you gamble for fun, you've already won." Yeah, right!

My introduction to gambling, much like smoking, came at a young age —far too young to grasp the consequences. My first bet was with my father, who owned horses while I was growing up. It was my 8th or 9th birthday at Aqueduct Raceway. My dad occasionally took us to the track on Saturdays when his horse was running. As owners, we had access to the owner's suite, a world of three-piece suits, carving stations, and the winner's circle . It was a scene of luxury and excitement, far removed from the gritty image of gambling many people imagine.

That day, my dad let me place a small bet. I picked a horse, and when it crossed the finish line first, I turned $5 into $60. For a young kid, it was electrifying. The thrill of cheering on my pick, the rush of the winner's circle, and the pride of stashing that stack of cash in my sock drawer—it felt like easy money, the kind that hooks you before you even realize what's happening.

By the time I was a teenager, I was well versed on the excitement of gambling. It wasn't a destructive addiction, but it was ingrained in the culture around me. Gambling was treated as a harmless vice, so long as you didn't lose your head. To his credit, my dad often warned us about its dangers—how gambling could ruin lives if left unchecked. But it didn't matter. Gambling was fun, accessible, and everywhere. It was woven into the fabric of growing up in my world, as pervasive as cigarette smoking.

In high school, my friends and I played dice at lunch tables and at parties. We bought scratch-off lottery tickets from the local stationary store, even though we were underage. Two-dollar Bingo tickets became a regular indulgence. Gambling was a social activity, a shared thrill and we all loved to participate, but none of us stood a chance against its allure. 21st birthdays for all of us meant trips to the casino, in all its now legal age glory.

Then came the poker boom of 2003, when Chris Moneymaker's win at the World Series of Poker turned Texas Hold 'Em into a national obsession. The game, touted as "a minute to learn but a lifetime to master," became a staple at every social gathering. We hosted poker nights before heading out for the night, throwing in $10 or $20 buy-ins for the quick game of poker with friends. For most of us, it wasn't a profitable pastime—just something that augmented the atmosphere of hanging out with friends, but it quickly became a habit for us to put together a card game at any time we wished.

By 28, I had added sports gambling to the mix. Whether it was poker, scratch-off lottery tickets, or betting on professional and college sports, gambling was omnipresent in my life. It wasn't until years later that I realized how close I had come to crossing the line from casual fun to dangerous compulsion. The combination of access, expendable income, exposure, peer influence, and cultural normalization had set the stage for harmlessly "gambling for fun".

Avoiding the Worst

When it came to other vices, I was lucky—or maybe just stubborn. I never touched hard drugs. Despite their availability, I had no desire to experiment. I also had great friends around me who were just as unlikely to delve deep into the drug world. My lifelong friend, Tim Sini and I still to this day, talk about how we kept each other in check when it came to going down that path. That's not to say I was completely innocent of some transgression. Casual drinking and the occasional attempt at marijuana (which I hated) were as far as I went.

Nicotine and alcohol were legal and normalized, so they felt like less of a gamble, though their dangers were clear. Other substances, however—cocaine, LSD, heroin—never tempted me. I knew too well the potential consequences and had no interest in finding out firsthand.

That's not to say I wasn't exposed. Drugs were everywhere, especially in my 20s and early 30s. There were always people around me who used, and plenty of opportunities to try, but I avoided them entirely. Perhaps it was fear of the unknown, or perhaps it was the influence of my parents, who would have been devastated if I had crossed that line. Either way, I steered clear.

Looking back, it may have been a small miracle that I never delved into the hard stuff. Then, like now, I just had no interest.

Lessons Learned

Reflecting on my experiences, it's clear I never battled addiction in the way so many others have. Nicotine still has its grip on me, and gambling is something I must approach with caution, but I've been fortunate to avoid falling deeper into those traps. There were moments when I came close, especially with gambling. The compulsiveness and obsessiveness that often accompany it are forces I've felt firsthand. But as I got older, I developed the tools to recognize the line I couldn't afford to cross, I also had more to lose once I was married with children.

I also realized that I work hard for my money, and there's no thrill in gambling worth risking it all. Today, I can enjoy the entertainment factor without letting it consume me. When it's time to stop, I stop. Maybe I'm lucky, or maybe I've just had the right support systems in place—parents who taught the dangers, friends who shared my values, and my own aversion to the worst consequences.

These experiences, however, have given me a unique insight into the mechanics of addiction—how it hijacks the brain's reward systems, turning fleeting pleasure into long-term dependence. And while I've managed to keep casual and occasional dabbles from consuming my life, I understand how easily the line can blur between control and compulsion.

A Broader Perspective

Growing up, the influences around me shaped my early relationship with vices. From cigarettes and gambling to the normalization of substances like alcohol and marijuana, the pressures were constant. Misinformation, peer pressure, and cultural cues were everywhere, often overshadowing the warnings from parents and teachers. Even with the best intentions, my parents couldn't shield me from everything. I still remember confronting my mom about smoking, only to hear her say, "We didn't know it was bad for you when we started." But they knew by then, and stopping wasn't so simple.

Addiction is never simple. It doesn't yield to willpower alone, and it's not something you can just quit on a whim. I've seen its devastating effects in others, from gambling to opioids, cocaine, and designer drugs. These addictions are ravaging lives on a scale far greater than what I've experienced.

My journey has taught me that addiction is universal, but so is resilience. With the right support, education, and self-awareness, it's possible to navigate the challenges and emerge stronger. I've avoided the worst, but I know how easily things could have been different. And that's why I'll never take my story—or my brush with addiction for granted.

Understanding addiction as both a personal struggle and a societal crisis would eventually cause me to act. As an educator, I've spent years working to empower young people with the knowledge and tools to make better choices.

As a father, my perspective is even more urgent. I see the challenges my children face—how the world they're growing up in is awash with addictive forces. Whether it's social media, online gaming, vaping, or the ever-present specter of stronger substances, the risks are omnipresent. My role as a parent is to guide, protect, and prepare them, but I also know I can't shield them from everything. What I can do, however, is equip them with the critical thinking skills and resilience to navigate these challenges and make better choices.

This dual role—educator and father—has solidified my commitment to combating addiction at its roots. I've learned that prevention starts with education, but it doesn't end there. It requires a holistic approach that includes community involvement, policy advocacy, and a relentless focus on addressing the underlying issues that fuel addiction, such as mental health struggles and socio-economic disparities. All of these realizations came to me when it was time to address my anxiety, with a little help from a friend.

15

F. ROBERT MAURIO

After the walk around the deck incident, I told Melanie I would heed her advice and see a therapist, there was no turning back. So, into the car I went, and down the road I drove. I had no idea what I was in for, but how could I?

When I heard the word *psychologist* growing up, I pictured a man in a suit sitting in an office lined with bookshelves, complete with a couch and an egg timer. It was an amalgamation of Jason Seaver from *Growing Pains* and Robin Williams in *Good Will Hunting*. So, as I drove to my first appointment that August morning, I had a very clear mental image of what I was walking into.

The mind is a funny thing. It constructs these detailed expectations, and when reality strikes, you're left marveling at how off you were. Pulling into the office parking lot, I realized just how far off I had been.

Nestled on a side street just off Main Street in our small community, the building was tiny and unassuming—a two-story structure that looked more like a quaint bed-and-breakfast than a psychologist's office. The gravel parking lot crunched under the tires of my car with a distinct, awkward sound, like driving over a bed of eggshells. The parking lot was barely big enough for three cars, mine being one of them. Two spots over, a Ford F-150 stood parked, looking oddly out of place.

"Odd," I thought.

Walking inside, I was greeted by a narrow hallway that led to a staircase. No receptionist, no waiting area, no sign of life. Just the stairs. My only option was up.

The second floor was just as understated. Two small rooms on the left, a modest office on the right, and a tiny waiting room tucked beside it. The air smelled faintly of Yankee candles, and soft classical music played from an Alexa speaker on the floor. The vibe was calming, but it wasn't what I expected.

The space was empty. Not just quiet—empty. No receptionist. No other patients. No signs of anyone else in the building. But there was a clipboard on a small table with a note taped to it:

"Paul Vecchione, please fill out the paperwork and go into the waiting room. Dr. Maurio will be right with you."

It felt strange, but I followed the instructions. After filling out the forms, I found a seat in one of the three chairs lining the wall of the waiting room. An open window invited the humid, late-summer air inside, mixing with the smell of candles. I glanced around, reading the inspirational quotes plastered across the walls, all while wondering what I'd gotten myself into.

This wasn't what I had pictured at all.

For a moment, I considered leaving.

I stood up, ready to make my escape. "This isn't for me," I thought. Just then, the door across the hall opened.

Shit.

Out walked a tall, thin man, probably in his late 40s. He was wearing an unassuming, almost casual button-down shirt and casual khakis. His demeanor was calm, his voice soft and raspy.

"Paul?"

"Yes," I replied.

"I'm Dr. Maurio. Go right on in. I just need to make a quick phone call."

Gulp.

There was no turning back now. I crossed the hall, entered his office, and sat down in a chair, waiting for him to join me. My mind was racing.

What the hell am I doing here? Just be honest. What's the worst that can happen?

The wooden floor creaked under his footsteps as he approached. When he entered the room, I braced myself for what I thought was coming.

Here we go. Let's unravel my childhood trauma on a couch with an egg timer.

But there was no couch. No egg timer. No probing into the depths of my past.

Dr. Maurio didn't nuzzle himself deep in your mind, seeking out the childhood trauma that often brings out the need to see a psychologist. Good thing he didn't, because we would have been stuck there a while, no childhood trauma to speak of.

He didn't try to unravel my past to reveal the issues of the present. He didn't prescribe medicine or throw a myriad of medical jargon my way to explain what I was experiencing and why. Everything about Dr. Maurio was cordial, casual, and concise. He had a method to his madness that was so brilliantly executed that to this day, I am still in awe of it.

He wasn't my doctor, he was my coach. He was the eyes and ears on the ground of a pretty tumultuous time in my life, as I described it to him. He listened, offered perspective, and mystically put me in a frame of mind that I can only describe as constructive, purposeful, and understanding.

He was my biggest supporter, my professor, my coach, and my sounding board. He understood the way I was feeling simply by engaging in normal conversation. Moreover, he was training me to understand it at the same time. As an educator, I know all too well the importance of understanding something before you can solve it. Dr. Maurio was all of these things and then some. He was so good at it and never gave me any indication that he was the professional in the room, and I was his patient. Instead, it was he and I, on the same team, working together to solve issues impacting my life. His professional take on things and his ability to weave them in and out of our conversations made it so easy for me to understand what I was going through, how to approach it in a healthy, productive manner, and mostly, how to solve it, with relative ease. It was not what happened in the past that's causing this distress, no. It was what's happening today, and what are you going to do about it now? You couldn't give Dr. Maurio fluff, or bullshit attempts, or half-assed excuses. It was, "What are you going to do about it now?"

He taught me the incredible benefit of perspective. The power of hope, self-appreciation, self-deprecation, and reinforced my self-confidence, which, at the time, was on a brief hiatus .

Through our conversations, he knew that I was a stand up guy, buttoned up and riding the better side of life, all of my life. He knew that I worked for everything and was also lucky to have what I had, both past and present. He knew I was mentally sound and strong. Most importantly, he knew, and brilliantly broached with me the fact that I was experiencing anxiety because, for the first time in my life, the engine was overheating faster than I could cool it off. In just four years I had drastically changed my life, with permanent, stressful caveats that needed my constant attention and focus. He knew the anxiety I was experiencing was not only normal, but common and very fixable. Every single conversation with him entailed a story from him, for the sole purpose of putting everything into perspective. Sometimes it was nonchalant, sometimes it was targeted and purposeful. But every time I walked out of his office and back into the storm, the rains let up a bit, the wind subsided a bit, the waters calmed a bit, and the ship steered a bit more on course.

Sure, he had all the boilerplate recommendations to curb the onset of an anxiety attack, most of which I practiced, most notably, meditation and exercise. He had an in-house meditation specialist who was so good at his craft that it took only a few sessions for me to learn extremely effective strategies for overcoming the sudden panic attacks I was experiencing.

By the time year five rolled around, Dr. Maurio and I would spend the sessions just talking about normal day-to-day life, politics, the stock market, the state of education, etc. Like we were two old friends meeting for coffee. There was almost no quote-unquote "therapy" going on anymore. There didn't need to be. He had taught me so much about my life, my perspective, gratitude for my incredible fortune to be who I was, how I was, and who and what I had. He taught me the benefit of picking up a pen and writing about my day before I went to bed, the so-called "dumping the trash" method, and he taught me strategies to approach stressful situations, difficult people, and unforeseen "life happens". I had gained so much with Dr. Maurio, and our time together would come to an end, almost five years to the day it started.

I did it. I sought help for my anxiety and found it. I sought shelter from the storm and found it. I sought relief from uncertainty and beat it.

As Dr. Maurio described it, I just needed a tune-up. And I got it.

I can handle the 24/7 shots of life that never seem to end. Work, health, home, children, bills, chores, sleep deprivation that comes with young children, difficult situations and people, haters, and unexpected circumstances and curve balls that come with being a 45 year-old husband and father of three, full-time educator, business owner, brother, son, neighbor and friend.

I certainly don't have it all figured out, who does? But because I embraced the power of mental health help, and took the walk up those stairs in Dr. Maurio's office that warm August morning, I now have the armor and renewed confidence to handle what comes my way. For that, and those five years with F. Robert Maurio, and my ability and willingness to learn what he taught me, I am forever changed. I am forever better. I am forever happier, I am forever prepared, and I am forever grateful.

Confluence and a Call to Action

Here's the thing. As I've detailed throughout this story, adversity wasn't something I had to face until it showed up on my doorstep— every single day, 24/7. And when it did, I was unprepared. I didn't have the tools to handle it. That's not a complaint. I'll never bemoan the fact that my childhood and early adulthood were relatively smooth sailing. But when the inevitable stressors of life arrived, they came all at once, fast and furious, and I had no idea how to process them and quell the madness raging around me.

The truth is, none of what I experienced was extraordinary in the grand scheme of things. People get married every day. People have children every day, planned, unplanned, or more than they expected. People own homes, work multiple jobs to make ends meet, maintain their relationships, and try to provide for their families. My story is not unique.

What *was* unique, though, was the way it hit me. For someone who had cruised through life with relative ease, it felt like a baptism by fire. It was relentless. It was overwhelming. And it forced me to confront the uncomfortable truth that I wasn't equipped to handle it. I tried to tell myself I could figure it out on my own, but deep down, I knew better.

The stakes were high. The lives and safety of my children depended on me. The health of my marriage depended on me. My own physical and mental well-being depended on me. Ignoring the problem wasn't an option. Admitting I needed help wasn't a sign of weakness—it was strength out of necessity.

What I've come to realize is that this reluctance to seek help wasn't just my hang-up—it's part of a larger, punishing stigma surrounding mental health. For too long, we've been conditioned to see asking for help as a failure, as if acknowledging our struggles makes us less capable, less strong, less deserving. That's bullshit. Seeking help isn't a sign of weakness—it's a testament to strength. It's saying, *I care enough about myself and the people I love to do what it takes to get better.*

That's the lesson that took me far too long to learn, but once I did, it changed my life.

A Transformational Journey

Dr. Maurio taught me so much in our time together. He guided me through what felt like the worst of my days to that point, offering perspective, tools, and strategies that reshaped how I saw the world—and myself. He helped me understand that what I was going through wasn't uncommon or insurmountable. It was simply my storm, and storms can be weathered.

But he didn't just teach me how to survive the tumult. He taught me something far more powerful: *gratitude.*

At first, it felt almost dismissive—this idea that I should be grateful while struggling so profoundly. But gratitude didn't mean minimizing my difficulties. It meant finding clarity, recognizing the bigger picture, and appreciating all the good in my life even as I worked through the hard parts.

The perspective I gained from those sessions was invaluable. By the middle of our time together, I'd gone from simply coping with the chaos in my life to thinking about how I could use my experiences to help others. It was as if the pieces of my life—my years as an educator, my struggles, my triumphs—were falling into place, forming a clear picture of what I was meant to do next.

The educator in me couldn't ignore the crises raging across the country. Mental health issues were at an all-time high, and the opioid epidemic was devastating communities. I saw it in my classroom, in my community, in the headlines every day. I felt a call to action, a pull to use what I had learned to make a difference.

A Call to Action

Life is strange. I walked into therapy seeking help to manage stress. By the time I walked out for the last time, I had a plan that would add even more to my plate—but in the best possible way. I was going to use them to help others.

The lessons I learned from Dr. Maurio gave me the tools to empathize with and support others facing their own. I saw a clear path forward: I could take my experiences as a teacher, my understanding of mental health, my understanding of addiction, and the strategies I'd learned and put them to work in a new way.

It was something that I knew I could do, and it all fell into place at the same time. Everything I'd been through—my career, my marriage, my parenting journey, my battle with anxiety and brush up with addiction —had led me to this moment. It was time to take everything I'd learned and pay it forward.

This wasn't just about me anymore. It was about making a difference.

The day I walked out of Dr. Maurio's office for the last time, I started down a new path—a path that would allow me to take the hardest parts of my life and turn them into something meaningful. I'd found it was a way to help others find hope, healing, and perspective.

And for that, I'll always be grateful.

PART III

A GENERATION IN CRISIS

16

THE SUBTLE SHIFT

G rowing up in the 80s and 90s, my childhood was a blur of bike rides, pickup games, and impromptu adventures with the kids in my neighborhood. Back then, the world was our playground, and we took full advantage of it. A lot of my friends were into skateboarding, and I remember the first skateboard I owned, the coveted Tony Hawk. We used to ride through the streets until the streetlights came on—the universal signal that it was time to go home.

We were outside all day until the sun went down, and it was the way kids mastered the education of the streets. We didn't have workshops on conflict resolution or seminars on collaboration—we lived it. There was always competition, arguments, and conflicts among friends. Boys back then had fist fights over disagreements, then shook hands when it was over and resumed play, like nothing ever happened.

But today, when I look around, I don't see kids doing what we did. The streets are quiet. The parks are empty. The neighborhood kids aren't out playing manhunt or arguing over the rules of a backyard baseball game. Instead, their faces are lit by the glow of screens, and their thumbs are moving faster than their legs ever did. The culture of outdoor play—the one that defined my childhood and helped shape who I am—is disappearing before our eyes.

Let's face it: the world and childhood have changed. Kids today are logging more screen time than ever before—an average of seven hours a day, according to studies. That's seven hours where they're not running around, not interacting face-to-face, and not building the kind of skills that come from those real-world interactions. I'm not against technology—far from it. It's incredible what we can do with it, and it has undeniable benefits. But let's be real: we've traded connections for convenience, and our kids are paying the price.

Think about how kids communicate now. Instead of hashing things out in person, they're using text messages and emojis. Sure, it's efficient, but it's also hollow. They're not learning how to read body language, hear the nuance in someone's voice, or resolve conflicts face-to-face. When everything is filtered through a screen, the human element gets lost. And when that happens, kids are left feeling disconnected, even when they're more "connected" than ever.

The mental health consequences of all this screen time are concerning, to say the least. Depression and anxiety among kids have skyrocketed, and it's no coincidence. Social media, for all its promise of connection, often does the opposite. Kids are bombarded with everyone else's highlight reels—the perfect vacations, the perfect selfies, the perfect lives—and they compare it to their own messy, imperfect reality. It's a setup for feeling inadequate, like they're never enough and will never fit in.

Then there's cyberbullying, which wasn't even a term when I was a kid. Back then, bullying was confined to the schoolyard, and when you went home, you got a break. Now? It follows kids everywhere, 24/7, through their phones. There's no escape, no sanctuary, and it's taking a toll in ways we're only beginning to understand.

And let's not forget how screen time impacts learning. Kids today are distracted—plain and simple. Between notifications, games, and social media, their focus is constantly being pulled in a million directions. Add in the sleep deprivation caused by late-night screen use, and it's no wonder academic performance is slipping. It's a vicious cycle of distraction, poor performance, and stress.

It's hard not to compare the childhood I had to what kids are experiencing now. When I was a kid, outdoor play was a way of life, and it was where we built resilience, learned teamwork, and found a sense of belonging. Now, that sense of community is fading.

I have spent a considerable number of pages in this story talking about my childhood and upbringing for a reason. Nostalgia aside--we are all living through a dramatic shift in how our kids formulate conflict resolution and human-to-human connections. The decline of outdoor play has become a loss of what makes us who we are as humans. It's robbing kids of physical activity, social skills, and emotional well-being. And it's creating a generation that's more isolated, more anxious, and less prepared to navigate the real world, and I see it every single day.

The Changing American Family

Growing up, my family was the embodiment of what many would call the "traditional" American household. There were six of us—Mom, Dad, me, and my three siblings—living in a suburban home on Long Island. My dad worked a steady job, my mom ran the house like a well-oiled machine, and we sat down together for dinner almost every night. We weren't perfect—no family is—but there was a rhythm, a structure, a sense of reliability that defined us.

Holidays meant a house full of friends and family, the dining room table extended with every leaf available, and the kitchen brimming with food. Summers were for barbecues, baseball games, and family road trips. The family unit was a constant, an anchor, and while I didn't fully appreciate it then, it was the foundation for much of who I am today.

But that image of the "traditional" American family has changed. The nuclear family—Mom, Dad, two kids, maybe a dog—has skewed from the standard. It's being reshaped, redefined, and in some ways, completely revolutionized.

Today, families come in all forms: single-parent households, blended families, same-sex couples raising children, multigenerational homes, and cohabiting partners who choose not to marry. The U.S. Census shows that the number of children living with two married parents has dropped significantly over the past few decades. Meanwhile, the number of kids being raised by single parents, grandparents, or other family members has risen steadily.

When I think about my journey as a parent, it's clear that family life today is more complex than it has ever been. Melanie and I are raising three kids in a world that looks very different from the one we grew up in. Our kids' schedules are packed with activities, school obligations, and social commitments in ways that would've been unthinkable when I was a child. Back then, we just went outside, found the nearest group of kids, and played until the streetlights came on. Now, everything has to be scheduled, coordinated, and carefully balanced. I'm not sure when it officially hit the scene, but we never had "play dates" growing up; interactions with our friends just happened.

And let's not forget the economic pressures. The cost of living, especially in places like Long Island, has made it harder for families to maintain the lifestyle that was once considered the American Dream. Dual-income households are the norm because, frankly, they have to be. Melanie and I both work full-time, and at one point, I was working two jobs just to make sure we could keep the lights on, pay the mortgage, and still put something away for the kids' future. That wasn't unusual—it was necessary.

Technology has also changed the way families interact. I can't help but remember how different dinnertime was in my house growing up. No phones, no distractions—just the six of us, talking about our days and occasionally throwing food at each other when things got rowdy. Now, I have to make a conscious effort to enforce "no screens at the table" rules. As my kids grow and navigate the fast-paced information and communication world we live in, understanding that technology has made our lives easier in so many ways, it's another challenge to navigate as a parent.

Cultural shifts have also redefined what family means. Same-sex couples can now marry and adopt children—a reality that wasn't even on the radar when I was growing up. Each of my kids has friends growing up in same sex households, and teaching acceptance and tolerance is something Melanie and I take significant strides to accomplish.

Divorce, once stigmatized, is now recognized as a necessary path for many people to find happiness and stability. Even the idea of gender roles within families has evolved. Melanie and I share responsibilities in ways that would've seemed unconventional a generation ago. She's just as likely to be fixing something around the house as I am to cook dinner or fold laundry.

The traditional breadwinner-homemaker dynamic has given way to partnerships where roles are more fluid. It's no longer about who does what. It's about what works best for the family. That's a lesson I've learned firsthand in my marriage. We've had to adapt, adjust, and compromise as we've built our lives together. And honestly, it's made us stronger, despite the challenges and chaos of our daily lives.

For all the ways the American family has changed, one thing has stayed the same: the core values that hold it together. Love, support, and resilience are constants, no matter the structure of the family. Whether it's a single parent raising kids on their own, grandparents stepping in to provide stability, or blended families navigating new dynamics, the essence of family remains. Yet the challenges faced by many children are inherently new in the American landscape, challenges that simply cannot be ignored.

I've seen this in my own life. My family growing up was far from perfect, but it was built on love and shared experiences. The family I've built with Melanie is the same. Yes, the challenges are different, but the foundation is unchanged. We want our kids to feel loved, supported, and prepared for the world, just as our parents wanted for us. The American family is evolving, and that's not a bad thing. It reflects the diversity, resilience, and adaptability of our society. But it also presents new challenges—economic, social, and emotional—that we need to address. We need to support all types of families, and while we embrace the changing American family landscape, we also need to recognize the challenges we face when it comes to our children. Family is still a unit, even if it looks much different today than it ever was, and our children deserve our steadfast efforts to embrace this reality and support it.

The Unseen Weight on Our Kids

I'm willing to guess that if you are around my age, you would agree that growing up, life felt simpler. My siblings and I had plenty of challenges, sure, but the pressures we faced were largely confined to the walls of our home, our classrooms, and the neighborhood streets where we played. The biggest worries for us were getting decent grades, belonging to a group of like-minded friends, and maybe catching a little heat from our parents when we stepped out of line. But today, kids are carrying a weight that's hard to even comprehend—a pressure cooker of expectations and exposure that never seems to let up.

Take academics, for instance. Kids today are being groomed for college from kindergarten. They're told they need perfect GPAs, Advanced Placement classes, extracurricular activities, and volunteer hours just to have a shot at being "competitive." Teachers, under enormous pressure from expectations and policies from above, have to pile on the workload as standardized tests loom large, and the constant drumbeat of "what's next?" starts earlier and earlier. It's relentless. I see it firsthand in my work with teenagers—they are burning out before they even get a chance to hit their stride. Learning has become a sidebar to unfair expectations that water down responsibilities and the accountability of our students.

Then there's athletics. It's no longer about playing a game for the love of it. Now, kids are being scouted for travel teams before they get to experience the fun of playing and learning a sport they love. Parents are investing thousands of dollars in private coaches, specialized camps, and the hope that their kid will earn a scholarship or make it to the pros. The joy of playing, of being part of a team, often gets lost in the chase for perfection. And if you're not the best? The message is clear: you're falling behind, and the effect on their sense of achievement and belonging on a team gets lost, to the detriment of their self-esteem and confidence. Youth sports, like life in general, are supposed to be a forum for kids to learn the value of teamwork, competition, failure, and resilience. There's nothing wrong with encouraging kids to strive for excellence, but here's a reality check for parents: the odds of your child becoming a professional athlete are slim to none. Too often, the messages we send our kids, starting at younger and younger ages, distort the true purpose of youth sports. Let them enjoy it for what it's meant to be, not what you imagine it should become. Unrealistic expectations of a pro career only set them up for disappointment.

And let's not forget social media. This wasn't even on our radar when I was growing up, but today it's the air kids breathe. Every aspect of their lives is under a microscope, curated and edited for the approval of others. They're bombarded with filtered perfection, highlight reels of other people's lives that make their lives feel like they'll never measure up. The comparison game is constant, and the pace of information is dizzying. They're exposed to everything—violence, political unrest, sexual content, impossible image standards, and the pressures of going viral—all day long and at their fingertips.

I've seen the toll this takes. Kids are more anxious, more depressed, and more disconnected than ever before. Social media has become a battleground where self-esteem takes hit after hit. The need to be "on" all the time, to keep up with this fast-moving world, has left many of them feeling like they're drowning. And for some, the escape they seek comes in dangerous forms—substance abuse, self-harm, or worse.

17

THE SYSTEM IS BLINKING RED

B ut don't take my word for it. Living and observing the toll all of this is taking on our kids makes for an easy story to tell. But numbers don't lie. Data regarding the impact of these crises is clear:

Drug Overdose Deaths:

In 2023, the U.S. recorded over 100,000 drug overdose fatalities, maintaining its position as the global leader in overdose deaths. [1]

Synthetic opioids, especially fentanyl, have been major contributors to these deaths. [2]

Suicide Rates:

Suicide remains a critical concern in the U.S. In 2022, the age-adjusted suicide rate was 14.3 deaths per 100,000 individuals, marking a 1% increase from 2021. Males had a significantly higher rate (23.1) compared to females (5.9) [3]

Surge in Youth Mental Health Concerns

According to the *Centers for Disease Control and Prevention (CDC)*, nearly 1 in 5 children in the U.S. shows symptoms of a mental health disorder each year. • During the pandemic, mental health–related Emergency Department visits among adolescents increased by **31%** compared to 2019 levels. [4]

Rise in Substance Use Among Adolescents

Data from the *National Institute on Drug Abuse (NIDA)* indicates that illicit drug use among teens rose dramatically in the last few years. For instance, there was a **61%** increase in 8th graders experimenting with drugs over 5 years (preliminary 2021– 22 data). [5]

Monitoring the Future studies show vaping (nicotine and THC) is now one of the fastest-growing substance use behaviors among U.S. teens. [6]

The Old Way Isn't Working

It would be unfair to declare that these issues have been ignored. They haven't. Substance use disorders and mental health problems have been part of our society for centuries, and there have been countless attempts to address them appropriately. Growing up, the "This is your brain on drugs" commercial was a constant, along with "I learned it from watching you, dad". We had lengthy anti-drug, pro-wellness education throughout my school years. Posters on the walls, guest speakers, presentations, and real-life reminders of the dangers of drugs and the need to be strong mentally and emotionally.

But I can say unequivocally that these methods have, for the most part, failed. The United States and the rest of the world continue to grapple with considerably high overdose and suicide rates, particularly among teens. So, where did we go wrong?

For decades, the approach to substance abuse and addiction was as flawed as it was limited. The prevailing mindset viewed addiction primarily through the lens of criminality, not as a public health crisis. Instead of seeking to understand the underlying causes of addiction, the system relied on punishment. The "War on Drugs" painted addiction as a moral failing rather than a complex interplay of biology, psychology, and social circumstances. Thousands of lives were derailed not just by substance abuse but by the harsh penalties that often accompanied it—lives that might have been saved with proper intervention and care were instead lost to a system that punished rather than focused on prevention and treatment.

In schools, programs like *DARE* (Drug Abuse Resistance Education) were rolled out with great fanfare. The concept seemed simple enough: arm kids with information, scare them with worst-case scenarios, and encourage them to "just say no." But as the years passed, evidence showed that DARE, while well-intentioned, was largely ineffective. Kids weren't just "saying no"—in fact, many of them were turning to drugs anyway, often in response to the very mental health struggles that went unaddressed.

Compounding the issue was the cultural tendency to sweep mental health concerns under the rug. Emotional pain was seen as a sign of weakness, something to endure in silence. Depression, anxiety, trauma —these were personal burdens to bear, not societal problems to solve. As a result, countless individuals self-medicated, using substances to dull the pain that no one would acknowledge. It was a cycle—unseen mental health struggles feeding addiction, and addiction feeding the stigma that kept those struggles hidden.

It became increasingly clear that the old ways weren't working. Criminalizing addiction didn't reduce it—it only deepened the crisis. Programs like DARE, with their one-size-fits-all scare tactics, failed to address the root causes of substance abuse or provide meaningful tools for prevention. And the stigma around mental health created a culture where seeking help felt impossible, even when it was desperately needed.

This growing awareness hit home for me on both a professional and personal level. I had seen the cracks in the system firsthand through my work as an educator, my mental health journey, and my observations of the broader cultural failings around addiction and mental health. But I was fortunate enough to identify and address the problem. I realized that I had the tools to be part of the solution. The lessons I had learned, the perspective I had gained, and my experience working with young people gave me the foundation to take meaningful action.

Action that was echoed by officials everywhere:

Calls for Mental Health Support by Education Officials

In a 2021 statement, *U.S. Secretary of Education Miguel Cardona* emphasized the need for comprehensive mental health services in K–12 settings, urging districts to invest in prevention and early intervention programs. Multiple state education agencies have begun rolling out competitive grants specifically targeting mental health innovations.[7]

Legislative Support for Mental Health and School Safety

The Safer Communities Act of 2021 emphasizes significant investments in school-based mental health services and crisis intervention programs. It aims to improve access to student mental health resources and enhance school safety, directly supporting initiatives like Prep Academy's comprehensive approach.[8]

Increased Demand for SEL & Whole-Child Approaches

Education Week Research Center found that **93%** of teachers believe social-emotional learning is either "very important" or "extremely important" for students' education. Many states now require schools to incorporate SEL standards, creating a **larger addressable market** for integrated mental health and substance abuse prevention programs.[9]

Importance of Early Intervention

The American Academy of Pediatrics declared a national emergency in child and adolescent mental health, stressing early detection of risk factors to prevent crises. Data shows that early identification and consistent follow-up can **reduce severe outcomes** (e.g., self-harm, overdoses) by up to 50%.[10]

School District Spending on Health & Wellness

A *2019 ASBO International* (Association of School Business Officials) survey reported that **68%** of districts plan to increase budgets for student wellness and prevention programs. Post-pandemic relief funding (e.g., ESSER funds) has allowed many districts to invest in new mental health or SEL initiatives.[11]

Teacher Burnout & Need for PD

National Education Association (NEA) surveys show increasing teacher burnout rates— over **55%** of teachers reported considering leaving the profession. Schools are seeking professional development offerings that equip teachers with mental health support skills—an area Prep Academy can address with its "Knowledge Is Power!" modules. [12]

Efficacy of Technology-Enhanced SEL

Collaborative for Academic, Social, and Emotional Learning (CASEL) states that well-implemented SEL programs can lead to an **11%** improvement in academic performance. Technology-based SEL interventions have shown promising results in pilot studies, further legitimizing edtech for wellness initiatives. [13]

With this new reality and the call to action palpable, I realized that a new, multifaceted approach to addressing addiction and mental health was urgently needed, which brought me to the conclusion that I had all that was necessary to address these crises effectively. Bring on **Long Island Prevention and Resilience Enrichment Program (PREP)**

PART IV

EFFECTIVE SOLUTIONS

18

LONG ISLAND PREVENTION AND RESILIENCE ENRICHMENT PROGRAM (PREP)

WWW.LONGISLANDPREP.ORG

O kay, I know what you are thinking! What the hell was *I* thinking? Naming my organization to combat teen drug misuse and address mental health awareness could have probably gone better. But let's face it—Long Island Prevention and Resilience Enrichment Program (PREP) takes up half a page, and the acronym? Let's just say I've had more than one colleague remind me it sounds like something you do before a colonoscopy. It's long-winded, clunky, and—let's not forget—geographically boxed in.

When I first came up with it, I didn't know the "Long Island" part would end up being a barrier, making it harder to expand and integrate outside the region. Rookie mistake. But here's the thing: I don't spend much time dwelling on regrets. I've never been one to waste energy on "what-ifs," unless, of course, Doc Brown and Marty McFly are swinging by with the DeLorean. What's done is done, and the name, though imperfect, is a small price to pay for what the program stands for.

Here's what I do know: I couldn't be prouder of *why* I created Long Island PREP and *who* it was created for. Kids. Kids, their parents, and their teachers. The name may not roll off the tongue, but the purpose is solid. It's about helping the next generation build resilience, navigate challenges, and grow into strong, healthy adults. If I could go back and change the name, I probably would. But there isn't a chance in hell I'd ever change its mission or its heart.

And maybe that's the point. Long Island PREP isn't about looking back; it's about the future. It's about the kids who will inherit this world, and the tools we can give them to face it head-on. It's about stakeholders handing the keys to the next generation and about how that generation will be better and stronger than the past.

Since Long Island PREP's inception in 2017, I knew from the beginning that it was important for me to go all in. Many times I thought of something I wanted to do but didn't follow through. Maybe the time wasn't right, or I lost the motivation due to unforeseen circumstances. But if I was going to spend the time, energy, and money to create something impactful, I was going to see it through.

Everything you've read thus far in this story has its roots in the Long Island PREP tree. From my childhood and upbringing and the many bumps along the way, the path to becoming a teacher, the students I taught and their stories, the tragedies in my and neighboring communities, drug overdoses and suicides, the 5k runs and foundations and amazing people I've met along the way to my battles with stress and anxiety to my decision to seek help and conquer it.

I think I was always chasing the big project, but could never put all of the pieces together. With Dr. Maurio's help, I was able to find the clarity I was lacking and found a way to make sense of what was happening in my life and communities across the country, and how I could light the fire of my ambition to do something special to help others. Long Island PREP was it.

While there is certainly ample research that indicates the urgent need for a concerted effort to address teen substance abuse and addiction and mental health awareness, I realized quickly that I needed to stay in my lane. I am not a psychologist or any kind of mental health professional. I am not a drug and alcohol counselor or rehabilitation specialist. There are specific, professional fields and niches for mental health and substance abuse issues, and I fit into none of them.

My dad, being a business owner himself, gave me the best advice I had received while trying to create an organization that would be costly and time-consuming:

"Do what you know the most and do what you love the most."

It made sense. I love teaching kids and disseminating knowledge, and helping parents guide their kids. I love helping people, and I love being the source of strength for people who need it. Maybe I couldn't offer professional help for those suffering from addiction and mental health issues. But I could absolutely make a difference by doing what I knew and loved the most: teaching and helping people.

I could pass along the knowledge of the causes and factors, and drivers of drug use and mental health, as well as effective strategies for prevention. "Knowledge Is Power" became a rallying cry for the organization because when kids and adults know what's out there, endangering kids, they are armed with the knowledge to stop it. When problem behaviors are identified, strategies for intervention could be applied to prevent nefarious behaviors from manifesting into destructive decisions. Educating the public at large and implementing interventions to change the course of children in crisis were both things I could do and do well. With effective adult awareness education, I knew I could bridge the glaring gaps of vital information about a child struggling between the school and home environment.. These were all things in my lane, and the integration of these strategies and the core philosophy of Long Island PREP would follow this course.

Maybe I might cringe at the name from time to time, but each word in that title was chosen with purpose.

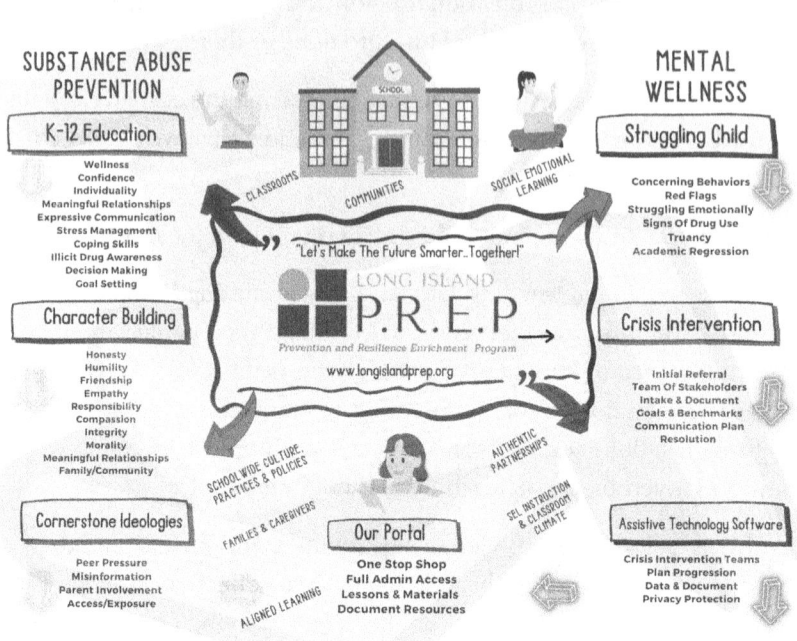

Prevention: The effects of substance abuse and mental distress can be devastating. They can ruin an individual's lives, their families', and futures. Many experts would argue that treatment for these issues, notably substance abuse and addiction, can be extremely difficult. I recognize that addressing substance abuse and mental health struggles requires more than just reactive measures. Instead, our programs emphasize the power of proactive education, equipping students, educators, and communities with the tools they need to identify and address challenges before they escalate. The word "Prevention" in the acronym serves as a reminder of this essential first step toward safe-guarding the well-being of our kids. Prevention may not be a novel concept, but I am a strong believer in the need for our society to address these issues with an entirely new approach. Part of steering kids down the right path is preventing them from going down the wrong path to begin with.

Resilience: Building *resilience* is another foundational pillar of the organization. It represents the ability to adapt and thrive despite adversity—a skill that is critical for students navigating the pressures of modern life. The inclusion of "Resilience" in the title underscores the belief that education is not only about academic achievement but also about instilling strength and perseverance in the face of personal and societal challenges.

Enrichment: Education has always been a central focus of Long Island PREP, but it goes far beyond conventional learning. Our programs prioritize *enrichment-based education,* integrating creative approaches, interactive methods, and personalized strategies to foster deeper understanding and engagement. By enriching education with innovative tools and experiences, students and educators are empowered to learn in ways that inspire and resonate. The inclusion of enrichment in Long Island PREP's approach reflects the understanding that prevention and resilience alone cannot fully prepare individuals for life's challenges. True preparation means enabling individuals to explore their passions, develop their talents, and find joy and meaning in their lives. Enrichment ensures that every program participant has access to experiences that enhance their mental, emotional, and social development, creating a more fulfilling and balanced future as powerful deterrents to drug and alcohol use and deleterious emotional outcomes.

The Spirit of Partnership Throughout Our Programs

No meaningful change can occur in isolation, and this truth is embodied in the final component of the acronym: *Partnership.* Long Island PREP collaborates with schools, community organizations, and families, recognizing that collective effort is key to achieving sustainable impact. This emphasis on partnership reflects the organization's belief in unity as a catalyst for growth and resilience.

With communities across the United States emerging from the COVID-19 pandemic, the increased incidence of substance abuse and mental health comorbidities among our children has provided the unmistakable fact that our children are in crisis. Augmented by the rise in mass shootings, suicide, and overdose rates across our country, we are in dire need of new, comprehensive programs to address each of these issues with a sense of urgency unforeseen in our history. With substantial and comprehensive substance abuse prevention and mental health awareness programs lacking in our schools and our communities, Long Island PREP was founded under the basic principles of improving and enhancing our current approach to these crucially important issues for students in school and their parents, as well as members of our communities.

We want to champion a new approach toward substance abuse and addiction through:

- **Early identification and intervention** - Assisting parents and crisis intervention teams in schools by creating and implementing individualized communicative and interventive prevention and student management plans, giving parents the power of choice when it is discovered that a child is in crisis.
- **Substance Abuse Prevention Education** - Empowering kids to embrace healthy choices by building self-esteem and confidence, and the necessary tools they need to resist drugs.
- **Public Awareness** - Educating, training, and assisting parents and professionals regarding the effects, factors, and dangers of drugs and alcohol.
- **Vigilance** - Learning from the past to safeguard the future.

Our philosophy is driven by the premise that information is the predominant factor in solutions, and an informed public is an empowered public.

- Children need to have the tools to resist drugs and alcohol. We strive to build their self-esteem and confidence so they can embrace the strength to do so.

Parents need the power of choice and individual focus on the needs of their children.

- We all need to learn from past mistakes and safeguard the future. Let us all be vigilant.

Cornerstone Ideologies

Our cornerstone ideologies make up the foundation of the programs. They are a holistic approach to addressing the teen substance abuse and mental health crises. At the heart of this approach are four cornerstone ideologies: **Peer Pressure, Misinformation, Access and Exposure,** and **Parent Involvement.**

These foundational concepts are not only the backbone of our programs but also seamlessly interwoven into every initiative we undertake. Together, they create a unified strategy for inspiring change and empowering communities with a focus on the root cause of teen substance misuse as the roadmap for effective prevention strategies.

Peer Pressure: a dominant force in adolescent behavior, often steering young people toward risky decisions, including substance use. By understanding the mechanisms of peer pressure, we aim to equip students with the confidence and skills to make independent, informed choices. Students need to build and solidify the strength to resist peer pressure.

Misinformation: Adolescents are inundated with mixed messages about drugs, alcohol, and mental health, often through social media and peer conversations. Misinformation leads to dangerous misconceptions, such as believing that certain substances are harmless or that mental health struggles are a sign of weakness. Students need to be able to identify and decipher misconceptions and misinformation regarding illicit substances, and build and solidify strong resistance to their influence on the intent to use drugs amongst teens.

Access and Exposure: The likelihood of substance use increases with availability and normalization. Environments where drugs, alcohol, or unhealthy coping mechanisms are prevalent make it easier for teens to engage in risky behaviors. Kids need to be aware of these facts and have the tools needed to resist use and limit their exposure by recognizing the people and influences among them.

Parent Involvement: Parents and caregivers play a pivotal role in shaping their children's attitudes toward substance use and mental health. Open communication and consistent involvement are essential for reinforcing positive behaviors and creating a foundation of trust. Research indicates that parents hold the biggest sway over the actions of their children. Parental monitoring of social media, friends, and activities can be a crucial deterrent to substance use, as well as strong and healthy social/emotional relationships. Students need to be active participants in establishing relationships with parents and close family.

19

INTEGRATION AND PROGRESSION
OF TOPICS

L ong Island PREP's programs are designed with a seamless integration and progression of topics that ensure a comprehensive and impactful approach to substance abuse prevention and mental wellness. Beginning with foundational mental health practices, such as stress management and emotional regulation, the programs build toward advanced topics like coping strategies, decision-making, and long-term goal setting. Each stage is intentionally structured to deepen students' understanding and foster personal growth, providing them with the necessary tools to navigate challenges effectively. This progression not only strengthens core skills but also aligns with proven methodologies for reducing the risk of substance abuse and enhancing overall well-being.

At the core of all Long Island PREP programs are foundational concepts that support holistic student development and well-being. These include:

- Wellness
- Self-esteem and confidence
- Individuality
- Meaningful relationships

- Expressive communication
- Stress management
- Coping skills
- Illicit substance awareness
- Decision making
- Goal setting.

Wellness: the cornerstone of a healthy life, encompassing physical, emotional, and mental health. Our mission emphasizes creating balanced, thriving individuals who can navigate challenges with resilience.

Wellness serves as the foundation for both substance abuse prevention and mental health awareness. By fostering a holistic approach to health, encompassing physical, emotional, and mental well-being, wellness equips individuals to build resilience and manage challenges effectively. When wellness is prioritized, individuals are more likely to develop healthy routines, such as balanced nutrition, regular exercise, and adequate sleep, which collectively improve their capacity to cope with stress. These habits reduce the likelihood of turning to harmful substances as a form of self-medication or escape.

Mental health awareness is also deeply tied to wellness. Recognizing signs of emotional distress, understanding the value of seeking help, and cultivating practices like mindfulness and meditation enable individuals to maintain stability during difficult times. Wellness education empowers people to view their mental health as an integral part of their overall well-being, destigmatizing the idea of seeking support when needed.

Self-Esteem and Confidence: Strong self-esteem and confidence empower individuals to resist negative influences, embrace challenges, and pursue personal growth.

They are critical protective factors in substance abuse prevention and mental health awareness. Adolescents with high self-esteem are less likely to succumb to peer pressure or feel the need to experiment with substances to fit in or mask insecurities. Confidence enables young people to make informed, independent choices rather than following the crowd or adopting risky behaviors.

In the context of mental health, self-esteem acts as a buffer against feelings of worthlessness or hopelessness, which can lead to emotional struggles. When individuals believe in their abilities and value their uniqueness, they are more likely to seek help when needed and less likely to internalize negative experiences.

Individuality: Embracing individuality encourages students to value their unique qualities and resist conformity to unhealthy norms.

Recognizing and embracing individuality is a powerful tool in both substance abuse prevention and mental health awareness. Adolescents who understand and value their unique qualities are less likely to feel pressure to conform to potentially harmful social norms or behaviors. When students are encouraged to celebrate their individuality, they gain a sense of self-worth that makes them more resilient to external pressures.

In the context of mental health, individuality promotes acceptance and authenticity, reducing feelings of inadequacy or the need to mask emotions. By fostering a culture that celebrates differences, individuals are empowered to express themselves without fear of judgment, creating a safe space for vulnerability and growth.

Meaningful Relationships: Positive relationships provide support, accountability, and encouragement, serving as protective factors against substance abuse and mental health struggles.

Positive connections with family, friends, and mentors provide emotional support, guidance, and accountability, reducing the likelihood of engaging in risky behaviors. A strong support system helps individuals navigate challenges and reinforces the idea that they are not alone in their struggles.

In the context of mental health, meaningful relationships create a safety net that fosters open communication and emotional security. Trusted relationships encourage individuals to express their feelings, seek advice, and access professional help when necessary. The absence of meaningful connections, on the other hand, can lead to feelings of isolation, which are often risk factors for substance abuse and mental health issues.

Expressive Communication: The ability to express oneself effectively is crucial for resolving conflicts, asking for help, and building relationships.

It is a critical skill in substance abuse prevention and mental health awareness. The ability to articulate thoughts, emotions, and needs enables individuals to navigate conflicts, resist peer pressure, and seek help when necessary. Without this skill, misunderstandings and unresolved emotions can lead to frustration, isolation, or reliance on harmful coping mechanisms like substance use.

In the context of mental health, expressive communication fosters vulnerability and emotional release, both of which are essential for healing and growth. When individuals feel confident in expressing themselves, they are more likely to address their mental health needs proactively, reducing the stigma around seeking support.

Stress Management: Stress is a common trigger for unhealthy coping mechanisms, including substance use. Managing stress effectively is vital for long-term well-being.

It is a key factor in preventing substance abuse and supporting mental health. Adolescents often face stressors from academics, relationships, and social pressures, which can lead to unhealthy coping mechanisms, including substance use. Effective stress management strategies empower individuals to navigate these challenges without resorting to harmful behaviors.

In the context of mental health, managing stress reduces the risk of burnout, anxiety, and depression. Techniques such as mindfulness, relaxation exercises, and time management allow individuals to maintain emotional balance, even in high-pressure situations.

Coping Skills: Healthy coping mechanisms enable individuals to handle life's challenges without resorting to harmful behaviors.

Adolescents often encounter situations that test their emotional resilience, and without healthy coping mechanisms, they may turn to substances or other risky behaviors as an escape.

Coping skills also play a crucial role in mental health. They enable individuals to process emotions, recover from setbacks, and maintain equilibrium in times of stress. Healthy coping strategies—such as journaling, exercising, or seeking support—foster emotional intelligence and long-term resilience.

Illicit Substance Awareness: Understanding the risks associated with illicit substances is a fundamental component of prevention. Adolescents often encounter misinformation or glamorized portrayals of substance use, which can lead to experimentation and dependency. Education that highlights the physical, emotional, and social consequences of substance use helps counter these narratives.

In the context of mental health, understanding the link between substance use and emotional well-being is vital. Substances often exacerbate existing mental health issues, creating a dangerous cycle. The illicit substance awareness of our programs helps individuals recognize these risks and seek healthier coping methods.

Decision Making: Good decision-making skills empower individuals to navigate complex situations and prioritize long-term well-being.

These skills are a critical defense against substance abuse and poor mental health outcomes. Adolescents often face high-pressure situations where quick, informed decisions are necessary. Teaching them to evaluate options and consider consequences helps them avoid impulsive, risky choices.

In the context of mental health, decision-making fosters self-agency and encourages proactive steps toward well-being. Whether it's deciding to seek help or choosing a healthy coping strategy, strong decision-making skills empower individuals to take control of their mental health journey.

Goal Setting: Setting and achieving goals fosters a sense of purpose and direction, reducing the likelihood of engaging in harmful behaviors.

It provides a sense of purpose and direction, reducing the likelihood of substance use and supporting mental health. Clear, achievable goals motivate individuals to focus on positive outcomes, creating a buffer against negative influences.

In the context of mental health, goal setting fosters hope and a sense of accomplishment. Breaking larger objectives into manageable steps helps individuals navigate challenges and build momentum toward success, and reduces the daunting nature of large, unmanageable tasks.

20

KEY MENTAL HEALTH PRACTICES
AND STRATEGIES

 "Addictive behavior is avoidant behavior. A tacit admission that life has become too difficult to handle, fueled by personal inadequacies and a lack of effective coping skills, and an addiction is born."

— DR. FRANK R. MAURIO

The connection between mental wellness and substance use couldn't be more clear. Mental illness and substance abuse are deeply interconnected, often fueling and exacerbating each other in a vicious cycle.

Many individuals struggling with mental health disorders, such as anxiety, depression, or PTSD, turn to drugs or alcohol as a means of self-medication, seeking temporary relief from emotional pain. However, substance use can worsen mental health symptoms, leading to increased dependency and further psychological distress.

Conversely, chronic substance abuse can trigger or intensify mental illness by altering brain chemistry, impairing cognitive function, and increasing vulnerability to stress and trauma. Educating individuals about these connections and providing practical strategies for prevention and intervention can be a powerful approach to breaking this cycle.

Building upon the foundational concepts of wellness, resilience, and prevention, Long Island PREP emphasizes the importance of practical, actionable strategies to support mental health and emotional wellbeing. These strategies—journal writing, exercise, gratitude, acts of kindness, mindfulness, and meditation—are integral to our programs. They provide participants with tangible tools to navigate life's challenges while fostering a proactive approach to mental health care. By embedding these practices into our programs, Long Island PREP empowers individuals to build emotional strength, improve self-awareness, and sustain long-term mental wellness.

Journal Writing

Journal writing is a powerful tool for self-reflection and emotional processing. By putting thoughts and feelings into words, individuals can clarify their emotions, identify patterns, and gain insights into their mental state. Journaling fosters self-awareness, helping individuals process difficult experiences and reduce and eliminate mental clutter, thereby "emptying the trash" that lingers in the mind.

Exercise

Exercise is a proven method for improving mental health. Physical activity releases endorphins, which reduce stress, improve mood, and combat symptoms of anxiety and depression. It also boosts energy levels and improves sleep, both which are critical for overall wellbeing.

Gratitude

Practicing gratitude shifts focus from negativity to positive aspects of life, fostering optimism and emotional resilience.

Research shows that gratitude reduces stress, improves relationships, and enhances overall mental health by creating a more positive outlook.

Acts of Kindness

Performing acts of kindness boosts mental health by fostering a sense of connection and purpose. Helping others triggers the release of oxytocin, a hormone that promotes happiness and reduces stress. It also strengthens relationships and creates a positive ripple effect in communities.

Mindfulness and Meditation

Mindfulness is staying present and fully engaged in the current moment. It helps individuals manage stress, reduce anxiety, and increase self-awareness by encouraging them to focus on the here and now rather than dwelling on past regrets or future worries.

Meditation is a powerful tool for calming the mind, reducing stress, and enhancing emotional resilience. Regular meditation fosters relaxation, improves concentration, and promotes inner peace, which are critical for managing mental health challenges.

21

CHARACTER BUILDING THEMES AND SOCIAL EMOTIONAL LEARNING

R esearch has shown that connecting children with the main stakeholders in their lives at home, in school, and within their social ecosystem for these purposes can have significant deterrent factors for drug use/abuse and improve mental health well-being throughout the most tumultuous years of their lives, years when substance use is likely to onset. This ideology is based on CASEL's SEL Framework now widely used in communities nationwide.

Character-building plays a vital role in SEL by helping individuals understand their values, develop strong interpersonal skills, and navigate social challenges with integrity and emotional intelligence. These traits not only strengthen relationships and improve emotional health but also serve as critical protective factors against substance use and mental health struggles. When individuals are guided by strong character, they are better equipped to make positive choices, resist peer pressure, and seek out meaningful connections that support their well-being.

Long Island PREP's mission is built on a commitment to empowering individuals, fostering resilience, and addressing the root causes of substance abuse and mental health challenges. As we explore the cornerstones of mental health practices and their role in substance abuse prevention, it becomes evident that fostering emotional intelligence and resilience is only part of the equation. To truly empower individuals and create lasting change, we must also focus on **character-building themes** that shape how people interact with themselves, others, and the world around them. These themes—honesty, empathy, responsibility, compassion, morality, humility, friendship, meaningful connections, integrity, and family/community values—are fundamental to social-emotional learning (SEL).

The Role of Social-Emotional Learning in Prevention and Wellness

Honesty

Honesty is a cornerstone of social-emotional learning (SEL), fostering trust, authenticity, and self-awareness. It encourages individuals to take responsibility for their actions, learn from mistakes, and build deeper connections. A culture of honesty allows open communication, strengthening relationships and emotional resilience.

In substance abuse prevention, honesty helps individuals acknowledge struggles and seek support rather than resorting to harmful coping mechanisms. Transparent communication within families, peer groups, and communities creates opportunities for early intervention, reducing the likelihood of substance use. Similarly, in mental wellness, honesty promotes self-reflection and emotional transparency, helping individuals address stress, anxiety, and depression effectively.

Empathy

Empathy enhances emotional intelligence by teaching individuals to understand and share the feelings of others. It strengthens relationships, improves conflict resolution, and fosters inclusivity, creating environments where people feel valued and supported.

By promoting compassion and reducing isolation, empathy plays a key role in preventing substance use. Adolescents who recognize their peers' struggles are more likely to offer support, reducing the need for unhealthy coping mechanisms. In mental wellness, empathy nurtures strong support networks, easing feelings of loneliness and reinforcing resilience.

Responsibility

Taking responsibility for one's actions and decisions cultivates self-discipline, accountability, and reliability—critical components of SEL. It helps individuals understand their role in a community and make choices that contribute to collective well-being.

In substance abuse prevention, responsibility empowers individuals to make informed decisions and resist risky behaviors. It also promotes goal-setting and purpose, reducing the appeal of temporary escapes like drugs or alcohol. In mental wellness, a sense of responsibility encourages proactive self-care, seeking help when needed, and supporting others.

Compassion

Compassion fosters kindness, understanding, and a willingness to help others, strengthening relationships and enhancing social cohesion. It encourages people to consider the feelings of those around them, creating a supportive and inclusive environment.

In both prevention and wellness, compassion reduces isolation and rejection, key factors that can contribute to substance use. It also encourages open dialogue, making it easier for individuals to seek help without fear of judgment. Self-compassion plays an essential role in mental health, reducing self-criticism and promoting emotional healing.

Morality

A strong moral foundation guides individuals in making ethical decisions and distinguishing right from wrong. SEL fosters integrity, fairness, and respect, shaping responsible and principled behavior.

In preventing substance abuse, a well-defined moral compass helps individuals resist peer pressure and make choices aligned with their values. It also fosters accountability and self-respect. In mental wellness, morality provides clarity in navigating ethical dilemmas, reducing stress, and reinforcing a sense of purpose.

Humility

Humility encourages self-awareness, openness to learning, and appreciation of others' contributions. It promotes mutual respect, emotional intelligence, and a growth-oriented mindset.

Recognizing when to seek help is crucial in preventing substance abuse. Humility enables individuals to accept guidance rather than relying on substances as a coping mechanism. It also fosters resilience by reframing setbacks as opportunities for growth, enhancing emotional stability.

Friendship

Friendships develop essential social skills such as communication, cooperation, and emotional support. Positive peer relationships reduce loneliness and foster trust, empathy, and shared experiences.

Strong friendships serve as a protective factor against substance use, offering accountability and emotional support. Adolescents with supportive friendships are less likely to seek harmful coping mechanisms for social acceptance or stress relief. Healthy friendships also provide comfort and encouragement, strengthening mental well-being.

Meaningful Connections

Beyond surface-level interactions, meaningful connections establish deep emotional bonds built on trust and understanding. SEL emphasizes the importance of strong support systems, collaboration, and genuine relationships.

Feeling connected to others significantly reduces the risk of substance use, as individuals with strong emotional ties are less likely to engage in harmful behaviors. These connections also provide a sense of purpose and belonging, reducing loneliness and promoting emotional resilience.

Integrity

Integrity reinforces honesty, consistency, and adherence to personal values. It fosters trust, respect, and authenticity, serving as the foundation for ethical decision-making and strong relationships.

A strong sense of integrity helps individuals resist peer pressure and maintain self-respect, making it easier to make healthy choices. In mental wellness, integrity ensures that actions align with values, reducing inner conflict and promoting emotional stability.

Family and Community Values

Family and community values shape personal and social identity, instilling principles of respect, cooperation, and collective responsibility. They provide emotional security and a sense of belonging.

Strong family and community ties act as protective factors against substance use by offering stability and clear behavioral expectations. Engaging in shared activities strengthens these bonds, promoting trust and communication. In mental wellness, these connections serve as a vital support network, reducing isolation and fostering resilience in times of challenge.

22

IT TAKES A VILLAGE

C onnecting Stakeholders:

With the myriad of challenges our kids face—substance abuse, mental health struggles, bullying, and social pressures—each of these is not confined to home or school. These issues ripple across all facets of their lives, requiring a collaborative approach that engages every stakeholder: schools, homes, teachers, parents, and communities. Only through collective effort can we ensure that children are safe, adults are informed, and everyone is working toward the common goal of substance abuse prevention and mental health awareness.

Shared Responsibility

Every stakeholder in a child's life plays a unique and vital role in their development. Schools are the primary environment where children learn not just academics but also critical life skills, social norms, and emotional regulation. Teachers are often the first to notice changes in behavior or signs of distress, making them key players in identifying and addressing issues early. Parents, on the other hand, are the bedrock of a child's emotional and moral foundation, providing guidance, support, and the nurturing environment essential for growth. Communities extend this support network, offering resources, mentorship, and a sense of belonging that reinforces positive behaviors and resilience.

Despite these interconnected roles, there is often a disconnect among stakeholders. Parents may feel overwhelmed or unsure of how to approach sensitive topics like substance abuse or mental health. Teachers may lack the training or resources to address these issues effectively. Communities, while well-intentioned, may not have the infrastructure to provide consistent support. The result is a fragmented system where vital warning signs are missed, and opportunities for intervention are lost. Bridging these gaps is essential to creating a comprehensive safety net for our children.

The Importance of Collaboration

A unified approach starts with communication. Schools, parents, and communities must establish open lines of dialogue to share information, concerns, and strategies. This communication ensures that everyone is on the same page regarding the challenges children face and the best ways to address them. For example, when a school implements a substance abuse prevention program, parents should be involved not just as observers but as active participants. They should understand the curriculum, reinforce its lessons at home, and feel empowered to discuss these issues with their children.

Similarly, teachers and parents must work together to identify early warning signs of substance use or mental health struggles. Teachers might notice a child withdrawing in class or displaying erratic behavior, while parents may observe mood swings or changes in their child's social circle. When these observations are shared, a clearer picture emerges, enabling timely and effective intervention.

Communities also play a crucial role in this collaboration. They can provide resources such as counseling services, extracurricular programs, and educational workshops that complement the efforts of schools and families. Community organizations, religious institutions, and local businesses can work together to create environments that promote healthy behaviors and offer support for those in need. By fostering a culture of care, communities can reinforce the lessons children learn at home and in school.

Fostering Substance Abuse Prevention

When stakeholders work together, the message of substance abuse prevention becomes stronger and more consistent. Children are less likely to experiment with drugs or alcohol when they receive clear, unified messages from multiple sources. By addressing the root causes of substance abuse, such as stress, low self-esteem, and lack of support, stakeholders can create a protective shield around children. Collaborative efforts also ensure that children have access to accurate information about the risks of substance use, countering the misinformation they might encounter online or from peers.

Promoting Mental Health Awareness

Mental health awareness is another critical area where stakeholder collaboration is essential. The stigma surrounding mental health often prevents children and families from seeking help. By working together, schools, parents, and communities can normalize discussions about mental health and create an environment where seeking support is seen as a strength rather than a weakness.

Schools can lead the charge by incorporating mental health education into their curricula and training teachers to recognize signs of emotional distress. Parents can model healthy coping mechanisms and provide a safe space for their children to share their feelings. Communities can offer accessible mental health services, support groups, and public awareness campaigns that reduce stigma and encourage early intervention.

When these efforts are aligned, children benefit from a robust support system that addresses their mental health needs holistically. They learn to recognize their emotions, develop healthy coping strategies, and seek help when needed. This proactive approach not only improves their mental health but also reduces the risk of turning to substances as a way to cope with unaddressed emotional pain.

23

PUTTING THEORY INTO PRACTICE

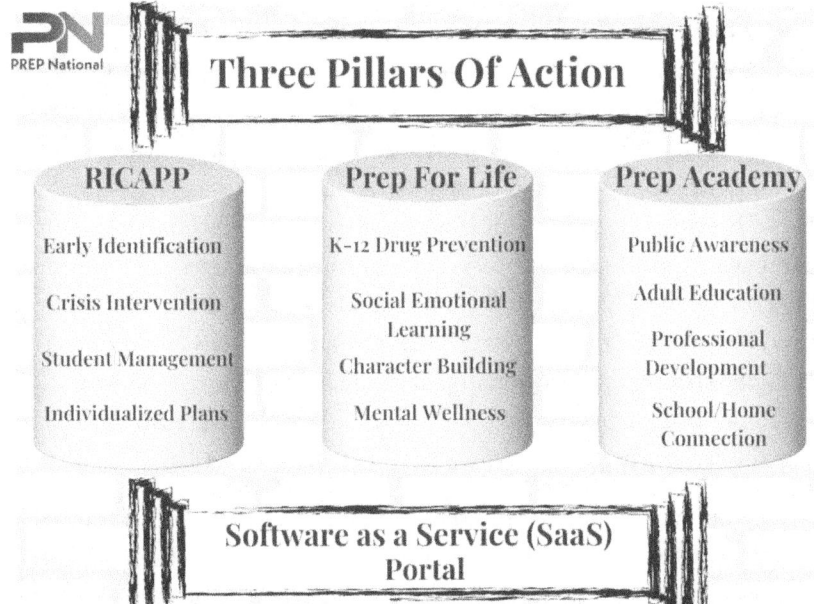

The Three Pillars Of Action

The stakes could not be higher. The challenges children face today —whether related to substance abuse or mental health—require an all-hands-on-deck approach. By uniting schools, homes, teachers, parents, and communities, we create a network of support that empowers children to thrive, and Long Island PREP has actively taken the initiative to make this happen. At the heart of our approach is what we call the "Three Pillars of Action." At the root of each pillar are Long Island PREP's cornerstone ideologies, key mental health strategies, character-building themes, and integration and progression of topics, an all-encompassing approach for children, parents, educators, and community members.

Pillar #1-- RICAPP

The first and arguably most critical of these is **RICAPP: the Recurring Individualized Communicative Addiction Prevention Program**. **RICAPP**, a centralized extension of schools' **Instructional Support Teams (IST), Response to Intervention (RtI), and Multi-Tiered Systems of Support (MTSS)** teams, specifically targeting substance abuse prevention and social emotional wellness through structured awareness, specific goals, intervention resources, and effective communication plans. These programs are already integrated into schools, providing a framework that **RICAPP** enhances by ensuring that students struggling emotionally or with substance use or at risk of developing substance-related issues receive timely, individualized, and coordinated support.

By extending and enhancing **IST, RtI, and MTSS**, **RICAPP** strengthens schools' existing student support structures, making them more proactive and effective in addressing children in crisis before they escalate. Rooted in collaboration, early intervention, and research-driven strategies, it provides a proactive framework for identifying and supporting at-risk students, offering a lifeline for students and a guide for educators, caregivers, and intervention teams working to create meaningful change.

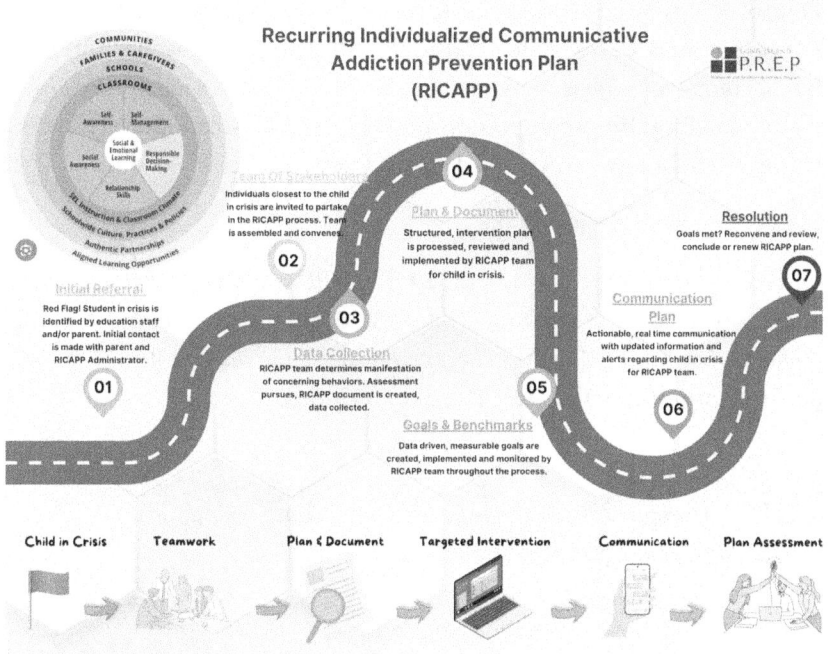

The Core Philosophy of RICAPP: From Red Flag to Resolution

At its heart, RICAPP operates on a simple but powerful philosophy: **early identification and intervention, student management plans for at-risk students that strengthen mental health practices to prevent substance abuse.** These two challenges are intrinsically linked, and addressing the emotional and mental well-being of students is a cornerstone for long-term prevention. By seamlessly integrating into existing school frameworks for crisis intervention teams, RICAPP creates a unified, structured approach that encourages open communication and collaboration.

This program isn't about reacting to crises after they've unfolded. It's about preventing them by identifying risk factors early and providing the tools and support necessary for students to thrive.

Key Aspects of RICAPP

1. Early Identification

One of RICAPP's standout features is its ability to detect potential issues before they escalate. Using a combination of teacher observations, counselor assessments, and data-driven tools, crisis intervention teams, collaborating with parents and stakeholders, can identify at-risk students and address their needs proactively.

2. Collaborative Action Plans

Once an at-risk student is identified, RICAPP brings together a team of educators, counselors, administrators, and caregivers. This team works collaboratively to develop an individualized plan tailored to the student's unique challenges. The plan includes:

- Initial Referrals
- Identifying problem behaviors through data collection
- Strategies for intervention
- Clear goals and benchmarks
- Regular follow-ups to ensure progress

3. Comprehensive Communication

RICAPP emphasizes seamless communication among all stakeholders. A centralized software as a service (SaaS) platform allows team members to share updates, discuss strategies, and track the student's progress in real-time. This ensures that no one is left out of the loop and that the student receives consistent support from all sides.

4. Structured Implementation

The program provides clear steps for executing the action plan:

- Assess the situation.
- Convene the team.
- Create a detailed plan with measurable goals, strategies, and benchmarks.
- Implement the plan with assigned roles and responsibilities.
- Track data and implement needed changes for optimal success
- Connect team members with real-time communication capabilities

- Conduct regular follow-ups to evaluate and adjust as needed.

5. Research-Driven Practices

Every aspect of RICAPP is rooted in evidence-based strategies, focusing on:

- Our Cornerstone Ideologies
- Our Key Mental Health Strategies
- Our Character Building Themes
- Our Integration and Progression of Topics
- Emotional regulation.
- Building resilience
- Strengthening peer and community connections
- Encouraging academic engagement

The Spark Behind RICAPP

My experience with students in crisis helped lay the groundwork for the development of RICAPP, most notably, Ryan. He was a student who appeared to have it all together—athletic, outgoing, and well-liked—but underneath, he was drowning. Considerable learning disabilities, parental pressure, and self-esteem issues compounded into a storm that almost overwhelmed him.

Ryan's case taught me the importance of structure, communication, and teamwork. When his struggles came to light, it wasn't just me who stepped in—it was a collective effort. His parents, coaches, the school psychologist, and I created a plan to address his academic challenges, communication barriers, and self-esteem issues. Together, we built a safety net that helped Ryan regain his footing and thrive.

That experience was transformative. It showed me that supporting a struggling student requires more than just good intentions. It takes a coordinated effort, a clear plan, and the willingness to adapt and respond to their evolving needs. RICAPP encapsulates all of those elements. It provides all stakeholders with targeted, data-driven intervention strategies to prevent nefarious behaviors from manifesting into destructive decisions.

Why RICAPP Matters

Students like Ryan are everywhere—kids who are struggling in silence, putting on a brave face while battling issues they feel too ashamed or overwhelmed to articulate. RICAPP exists to bridge that gap. It gives schools and parents the tools to:

- Spot the warning signs early.
- Create individualized and tailored, actionable plans.
- Foster collaboration among educators, families, and communities.
- Provide students with the structure and support they need to overcome challenges before they escalate.
- Provide crisis intervention teams and parents with goal-specific resources and proactive activities to address concerning behaviors.

By addressing substance abuse and mental health challenges through a holistic, research-backed approach, RICAPP is a game-changer. And for me, it's a way to ensure that every student has a team like Ryan's in their corner. Because when we work together, we can catch them before they fall—and set them on a path to success.

Pillar #2: Prep for Life: Empowerment Through Education

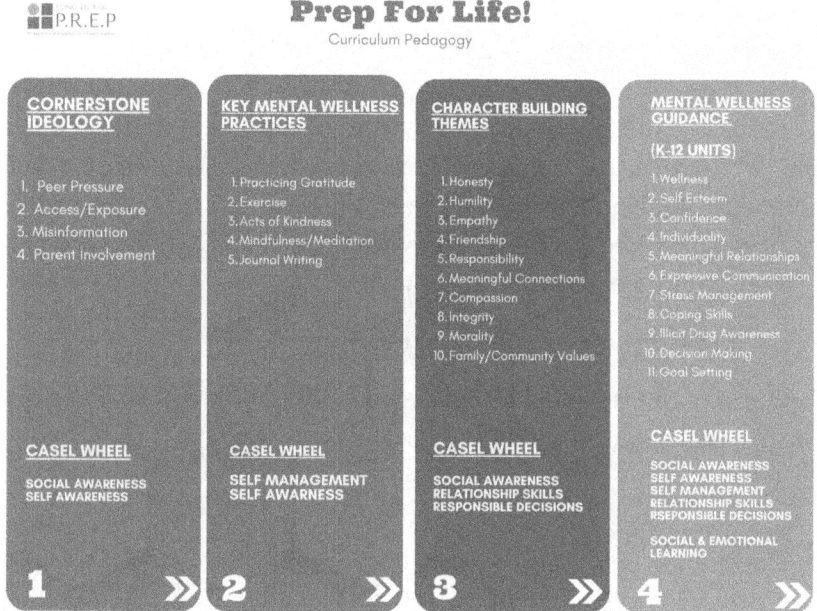

When I think about **Prep for Life**, the second pillar of Long Island Prep's mission, I can't help but think of Finn and PJ. Their stories are what make this program so personal to me. They are reminders that education reaches far beyond the classroom. It's about building resilience, fostering hope, and equipping kids with the tools they need to navigate the challenges of life. Finn and PJ taught me that as a teacher, I can help them navigate their challenges while instilling in them valuable life lessons to take with them.

The Philosophy Behind Prep for Life

The foundation of Prep for Life is simple: **knowledge is power.** When students are with the right tools and understanding, they're empowered to make better decisions and support each other. Finn and PJ's experiences showed me firsthand how much kids need a lifeline—a source of stability and encouragement in a world that often feels overwhelming. Prep for Life is built to be that lifeline because it grew out of experiences in the classroom with at-risk students.

Prep For Life is a K-12 curriculum designed to integrate substance abuse prevention and mental health awareness into everyday education. It's about reaching students where they are, helping them build the self-esteem and confidence to resist drugs with sound social emotional foundations, teaching them the dangers and consequences of destructive decisions, and showing them that they have what it takes to overcome whatever comes their way.

Embedded Concepts Across the Curriculum

Each lesson in Prep for Life includes foundational themes that address the real challenges kids face today, seamlessly integrating:

Our Cornerstone Ideologies:

Peer Pressure: Empowering students with decision-making strategies and confidence to resist negative influences and make independent, healthy choices.

Access Exposure: Educating students on the real-world availability of substances and risky behaviors, fostering awareness and proactive prevention.

Misinformation: Teaching critical thinking skills to help students identify false narratives, media influence, and misleading information related to substance use and mental health.

Parent Involvement: Providing resources and guidance to strengthen family communication, ensuring parents play an active role in prevention and support.

Our Key Mental Health Strategies:

Journaling: Encouraging self-reflection and emotional processing, helping students recognize patterns in their thoughts and develop healthier coping mechanisms.

Exercise: Promoting physical activity as a natural stress reliever, enhancing mood, reducing anxiety, and improving overall mental well-being.

Mindfulness and Meditation: Cultivating present-moment awareness, teaching students how to manage stress, regulate emotions, and build resilience through focused breathing and relaxation techniques.

Acts of Kindness: Reinforcing the power of compassion and connection, showing how small, positive actions can improve self-esteem, foster relationships, and enhance overall mental health.

Our Character Building Themes:

- **Honesty:** Encouraging truthfulness and transparency, fostering trust and strong character in personal and academic life.
- **Empathy:** Cultivating the ability to understand and share the feelings of others, strengthening relationships, and promoting emotional intelligence.
- **Responsibility:** Instilling accountability for actions, decisions, and commitments, empowering students to take ownership of their growth.
- **Compassion:** Promoting kindness and concern for others, encouraging students to support and uplift those in need.
- **Morality:** Reinforcing ethical decision-making and a strong sense of right and wrong in everyday life.
- **Humility:** Teaching self-awareness and the value of learning from others, fostering personal growth, and gratitude.
- **Friendship:** Highlighting the importance of loyalty, trust, and support in building lasting, meaningful relationships.
- **Meaningful Connections:** Emphasizing the power of authentic relationships in personal fulfillment and mental well-being.
- **Integrity:** Encouraging consistency between values and actions, promoting a strong moral compass, and reliability.
- **Family/Community Values:** Strengthening the importance of unity, support, and shared responsibility in shaping a positive society.

Integration and progression of topics:

- **Wellness:** Encouraging a balanced approach to physical, mental, and emotional health, fostering long-term well-being.
- **Self-Esteem and Confidence:** Building self-worth and resilience, empowering students to embrace their strengths and overcome challenges.
- **Individuality:** Celebrating personal uniqueness, encouraging students to embrace their identity and stand firm in their values.
- **Meaningful Relationships:** Reinforcing the importance of trust, respect, and mutual support in building lasting personal and professional connections.
- **Expressive Communication:** Developing the ability to articulate thoughts and emotions effectively, strengthening relationships, and reducing misunderstandings.
- **Stress Management:** Providing tools to navigate pressure and anxiety, promoting healthy habits for emotional balance and productivity.
- **Coping Skills:** Equipping students with strategies to handle adversity, ensuring they can manage challenges constructively and positively.
- **Illicit Substance Awareness:** Educating students on the risks and consequences of substance use, empowering them to make informed choices.
- **Decision Making:** Strengthening critical thinking and problem-solving skills, fostering responsible choices and long-term success.
- **Goal Setting:** Instilling the importance of ambition and perseverance, guiding students toward purposeful achievements and personal growth.

Lessons from Finn

When Finn handed me that crumpled note, it was so much more than a cry for help—it was a moment that changed everything for me. Finn was being crushed by the weight of bullying, low self-esteem, and personal struggles. The classroom was supposed to be a safe place, but for him, it often wasn't. I realized that beyond academics, what Finn needed most was **support, structure, and someone to believe in him.**

The work I did with Finn laid the groundwork for the **wellness, coping skills, and self-esteem** components of Prep for Life. It taught me that students need more than lessons—they need to know that someone cares, that their struggles matter, and that there's a path forward. Finn's journey also underscored the importance of involving support systems—parents, counselors, and teachers working together to create a plan for success.

Lessons from PJ

Then there was PJ, the quiet, kind-hearted student who wore his struggles like an invisible cloak. On the surface, he seemed fine, but underneath was a kid yearning for guidance and support. PJ's story is where I learned the importance of **mentorship and expressive communication**, helping kids find their voice and use it to process their emotions and experiences.

PJ didn't need me to solve his problems; he needed me to listen, guide, and encourage him to believe in himself. The **interactive journaling and goal-setting tools** in Prep for Life are a direct result of my time with PJ. I saw how writing and self-expression helped him work through his challenges, and I knew it could help other kids, too.

How Prep for Life Works

Prep for Life is designed to be flexible, engaging, and practical for today's classrooms. It offers:

- **Customizable lesson plans:** Teachers can adapt the program to fit their students' needs.
- **School-to-home connections:** Newsletters and resources help parents reinforce what's taught in school.
- **Interactive exercises:** Activities that promote teamwork, critical thinking, and self-reflection.

- **Journaling and goal-setting tools:** Encouraging students to express themselves and plan for the future.

Just like Finn and PJ needed tailored support, Prep for Life recognizes that every student is unique. The program is designed to meet kids where they are and give them the tools to succeed on their terms.

A Collaborative Effort

One of the key lessons I learned from Finn and PJ is that no one can do this alone. It takes a village to help kids thrive. That's why Prep for Life emphasizes collaboration between schools, parents, and communities. When everyone is on the same page, the impact is far greater.

Why Prep for Life Matters

Kids today are under more pressure than ever, and they're struggling in ways that aren't always visible. Prep for Life is about giving them the tools to thrive. It's about tying together the fabric of healthy choices and strategies to resist destructive decisions into their everyday education, while building the tools to be better for themselves and everyone around them.

Pillar #3: Knowledge is Power--: Bridging the Gap Between Home, School, and Community

Knowledge is Power is about more than sharing information—it's about empowering individuals and communities to take meaningful action together. This program stands as a critical bridge, connecting what parents observe at home with what teachers witness in the classroom. It's a unifying force that ensures all stakeholders are on the same page when it comes to understanding and addressing the complexities of teen substance abuse and mental health.

When I think about why **Knowledge is Power** is so vital, I think about Parker. His story exemplifies the importance of collaboration, understanding, and the transformative power of support systems. Parker served as a reminder of the power of education through collaboration and how it extends into building confidence, resilience, and a belief in one's potential that is born and fostered at home and reinforced with key figures in a child's life, including their teachers.

The Philosophy Behind Knowledge is Power

At its core, **Knowledge is Power** is based on a simple idea: education is the foundation of prevention. But this education must go beyond students—it needs to include adults, too. Parents, teachers, and community members all have a role to play in fostering environments where kids can thrive.

By equipping adults with the tools to recognize the signs of teen angst, understand the factors driving substance use and mental health challenges, and respond effectively, **Knowledge is Power** becomes the reinforcing element of Long Island PREP's **Three Pillars of Action**. It ties together the intervention-focused strategies of RICAPP and the prevention education curriculum of Prep for Life, creating a comprehensive framework for effective substance abuse prevention and mental wellness.

What Parker Taught Me

Parker's story is a testament to how vital it is to bridge the gap between what happens at home and what unfolds at school. His confidence and resilience were the attributes of his parents' efforts to instill a strong sense of self-worth and our work in school to reinforce those lessons.

But not every child has a Parker-like support system at home. Some parents may not fully understand the pressures their kids face or recognize the early signs of struggles with mental health or substance use. And teachers, while often keenly aware of these struggles in the classroom, may not know the full scope of what's happening at home or possess the tools and strategies to address them appropriately. This disconnect can leave kids without the unified support they need to succeed.

Knowledge is Power is designed to address this gap. It brings parents and teachers together, ensuring everyone involved in a child's life is informed, aligned, and empowered to make a difference.

Embedded Concepts in Knowledge is Power- Essential Adult Education, Including

- Our Cornerstone Ideologies
- Our Key Mental Health Strategies
- Our Character Building Themes
- Our Integration and Progression of Topics

These themes are central to every seminar, workshop, and resource in the program, ensuring that both adults and children are equipped to face challenges together.

Bridging School, Home, and Community

Knowledge is Power fosters collaboration by connecting parents, teachers, and community members and ensures that prevention efforts are comprehensive and cohesive. Specific strategies include:

- **School-to-Home Resources:** Providing parents with materials that reinforce lessons taught in school, ensuring consistency and alignment.
- **Collaborative Workshops:** Creating spaces where educators, parents, and community leaders can share insights and strategies.
- **Adult Education:** Offering seminars that delve into the factors driving teen angst, from academic pressures to social media influences, key factors, and warning signs of drug use and emotional struggles, empowering adults with the knowledge to better support the kids in their lives.
- **Ongoing Support:** Ensuring that resources and learning opportunities are available long after the workshops end.

Why Knowledge is Power Matters

The pressures on kids today are immense. **Knowledge is Power** equips the adults in children's lives to be a source of accurate information, strength, and guidance. It provides stakeholders with the foundation of effective partnership in keeping their kids safe by bridging the gap between home and school, and it ensures that kids don't have to navigate life's challenges alone.

Knowledge Is Power is offered through our "Prep Academy" and is an innovative online learning platform designed for schools, teachers, and professionals seeking expert-led education in substance abuse prevention, mental health awareness, and crisis intervention. It offers comprehensive training modules, professional development courses, and evidence-based strategies to equip educators and professionals with the tools they need to support students and communities. With flexible, on-demand access, PREP Academy ensures that knowledge leads to action, fostering safer, healthier environments nationwide.

www.theprepacedemy.com

Educating Our Educators, Parents and Professionals

PREP Academy offers an innovative online platform for professional development in Social and Emotional Learning (SEL), Mental Wellness, and Resistance to Substance Abuse. It targets educators, administrators, parents, and students, equipping them with evidence-based practices and tools to create healthier environments for young people. PREP Academy is recognized as an approved sponsor of Continuing Teacher and Leader Education (CTLE), facilitating ongoing professional growth for educators and leaders.

Participants can customize their learning to suit their needs, selecting from various courses that provide practical tools and resources for immediate application. The Academy focuses on supporting mental well-being as a key aspect of effective substance abuse resistance and social emotional learning.

www.theprepacademy.org

*Courses and Workshops may be In Person, Virtual or Asynchronous

ALL COURSES
Promoting Positive Mental Health in the Digital World

ALL COURSES
Understanding Social Media and It's Impact

ALL COURSES
Dangerous Trends

The Portal

For me, Long Island PREP's programs are about making sure the people who need it most can use it. In today's world, where everything moves fast and educators already have more on their plates than ever, access has to be easy. That's why every lesson, resource, and assessment is housed in our interactive Software-as-a-Service (SaaS) portal, giving schools, teachers, parents, and community leaders everything they need, exactly when they need it.

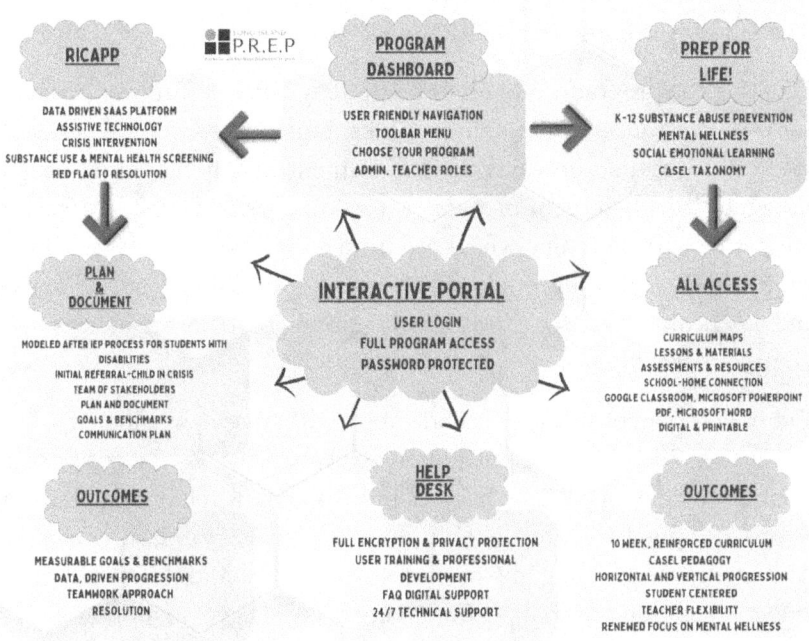

Let's be real, educators are already stretched thin, and expecting them to jump through hoops just to access critical content isn't realistic. So, we took that frustration out of the equation. With our digital platform, everything is right there at their fingertips—whether it's planning a lesson, tracking progress, or just looking for the right way to start an important conversation with a student.

Teachers have access to everything in their classrooms. Administrators can oversee implementation, parents can find guidance, and community leaders can tap into resources that help them support the kids they work with. We developed the portal to make things easier so that the focus stays where it belongs—on giving students the knowledge, skills, and support they need to navigate the real challenges they're facing.

At the end of the day, it's about making sure these programs get into the hands of the people who can use them to make a difference. And by putting everything in one place, accessible anytime, anywhere, the portal makes sure that happens.

The mission of Long Island PREP is **Worth The Fight**

Creating the programs offered through Long Island PREP was no small task—it was an enormous undertaking built on years of experience, dedication, and an unwavering commitment to helping young people navigate the challenges of today's world. These programs were not simply constructed; they were born from a lifetime of working directly with teens, witnessing firsthand their struggles with substance abuse, mental health, and the pressures of growing up in an increasingly complex society.

Every component of Long Island Prep's initiatives—whether it's *Prep for Life's* evidence-based prevention education, *RICAPP's* crisis intervention system, or *PREP Academy's* professional development platform—was designed with one goal in mind: to create real, lasting change. The work was grueling, the obstacles were many, and the system itself often felt resistant to change. But giving up was never an option.

Because at the heart of it all, this effort was about building a movement. A movement fueled by the belief that our kids deserve better. They deserve for schools to prioritize their mental health and implement effective substance abuse prevention programs. Their communities should equip them with the tools to make safe, informed choices. And they need adults who refuse to look the other way.

This work isn't finished—far from it. But as these programs continue to grow, reach more students, and impact more communities, they serve as proof that change is possible. And that a lifetime spent fighting for the well-being of young people is a fight always worth taking on.

24

WHY WE FIGHT

Throughout my journey, I've had the privilege of working with incredible people—those on the front lines of substance abuse and mental health crises. If there's one lesson I've learned, it's that we are all in this together. Every parent, teacher, and community member has a role to play in protecting our children and shaping a better future.

Of all the awareness seminars, speaking engagements, and workshops I've been part of, nothing has impacted me more than meeting the parents who have lost their children to these ongoing crises. Their grief is immeasurable, their loss irreplaceable—but their determination to help others and honor their children's legacies is profoundly inspiring. I've listened to their stories, felt their anguish, and, most of all, been moved by their unwavering mission to ensure their children did not die in vain.

It is an honor to share some of these stories with you. Stories of resilience, selflessness, and the hope that no other family will have to endure the same heartbreak.

May their voices serve as a reminder that we can all turn on a light in the darkness.

CJ Neumann

By Joy Neumann, his mother, and The Beat Lives On

"I love you more than life itself."

Charles Joseph Neumann was born on August 18th, 1991, he was my first-born child. A truly gentle soul with a contagious smile, and he gave the sweetest of hugs. I sheltered him in his early years. I admit, I didn't even let him ride his bike around the corner until he was fourteen years old. He had once shared with me that I protected him too much, but he was equally protective of me.

He had an easy-going nature and laid-back sense of humor that many times was often infused with lighthearted shenanigans.

One of his gifts was in music, where he naturally developed the skill to create catchy beats and began to hone his skills in music production. He graduated number one in a music production class he had taken in New York as a testament to his promise as a music producer.

CJ was loyal to his family; his character was an integral part of our family's togetherness. He was very loved and was always so welcoming.

These were the very things about him that created this eternal shock for all who knew him. "How could such a beastly addiction come upon this graceful, ingenious young man?" We all still rustle with that thought, especially standing at the foot of his tombstone.

"Bringing the dark to light"

When I found out my son CJ was doing heroin, it was beyond a mother's words what anguish and dire fear I felt, especially of a child who was deathly afraid of needles; he used to scream at the top of his lungs during doctor visits.

It was my younger son, Raymond, who came to me, suggesting that I look under CJ's mattress because he thinks he is doing drugs. When my husband and I acted on his comments, I remember seeing an elastic band and needles. He said it wasn't his at first, and I started to cry as my husband, RJ, asked him frantically, "CJ, what are you doing?" We promptly talked with him. I do not remember exactly what we discussed, but we had in our minds the fact that another kid in Lindenhurst had just passed away from a heroin overdose, so it was so very fresh in our minds and extremely upsetting.

Like for so many kids, drugs were all around him, and when friends succumb to its temptation, often the most unsuspecting individuals can get caught up in it as well. CJ started smoking Marijuana in high school, and as often can happen, where cannabis leads to other drugs, he somehow became addicted to opioids.

It remains a mystery today how that occurred, with only a horrendous rumor that someone stuck a needle in his arm at a party where he had supposedly passed out. Probably from some other substance or possibly alcohol, because he wasn't a drinker. He was a small-framed boy, so it wouldn't take much to take him down.

"He fell to the cruelty of the world within the shelter and comfort of his room."

It was a cloudy Tuesday morning, May 6^{th,} my mother's birthday. I was getting ready for work, going through my usual routine. I went into CJ's room to wake him up so he could get ready for a meeting. When I walked in, I think the first thing I saw was the needle at the edge of the bed, and CJ slumped over in a sitting position with his favorites next to him, a juice box and chicken on a stick.

I screamed; my husband was downstairs at the time, recovering from a recent knee surgery. I ran out of the room with the needle. I still don't know to this day why I had the needle in my hand. My husband hobbled upstairs as fast as he could, telling me to call 911. I went downstairs to call and shouted to him that they said, "Put your fingers under his nose to check and see if he is breathing."

I ran back upstairs and all I remember was my husband lifting him, he was stiff, I will never forget my son's face, and his eyes were open. After that, God must have stepped in because I went completely numb, an absolute state of shock, just walking around in circles. I was suddenly empty. I still have blocked out that day somehow, however, I can revisit it with much more strength these days.

When the paramedics arrived, they made us go downstairs as they tried to revive him, and they told us not to go upstairs. I was outside in the backyard when they carried him downstairs from his room.

When I came back in, my husband was sitting on the couch and began tugging on my arm to sit down, but it was completely numb, I couldn't sit, I just couldn't be there for him. The police officer approached us to tell us officially that he was gone, saying, "he must have passed sometime in the middle of the night." A "speed ball," as it is called on the streets, which is a lethal cocktail of drugs that must have been tainted, and his heart couldn't take it.

I would often tell CJ about drug deaths, and he would tell me why that probably happened. He would say what I believe is the street lingo, that "you must tell the dealer medium", he was aware of this. I find some faint comfort in knowing that he would have at least asked for that.

One of my deepest regrets is that I didn't get to hold him, but "thank God my husband was there that dreadful day."

"I came so close to saving my son as he came so close to saving himself."

CJ had to want to go to rehabilitation; to try and force an addict to go would be in vain. That's what makes his story a little different, along with the fact that he stayed away from unscrupulous activities often tied to addiction. One of his strengths in doing so was his obvious love, respect, and trust he had for me, that's the type of child he was.

For a time, CJ was always in his room, and he would sometimes say, "You don't want me out there." He was weaning himself off with Suboxone strips, which help an addict with their urges.

He had told me in an instant, during the withdrawal process, that it was "like a Mack truck had hit him." He suffered from nausea, dizziness, and other maladies common in a withdrawal phase. I gave him Imodium for diarrhea, Mezzanine for dizziness, whatever my motherly instinct and Google searches could summon up. Through those days, I witnessed how the physical affliction alone was taxing on the necessary mental stamina CJ would need to get him through this.

It was astonishing to me at one point when I had reached out to clinics for the Suboxone that they told me I had to "bring him in high" to receive treatment. "There was no way I could do that!"

I recall a day when I drove him to this house where he knew he could get some Suboxone because he was down to a small piece. I gave him $20 to do so and waited. CJ didn't want anyone to know about his addiction, and it was a dangerous state of mind because pride in these circumstances creates a greater challenge than one is already facing. Yet, somehow at the same time, he was trying to help others.

I still picture him to this day, standing there with his duffel bag at Seafield in Amityville, everything he was wearing with his quiet, shy disposition, one of his sweetest qualities, I was swallowed up in emotion.

It was about an hour or so that we sat in the waiting room, people were continually coming in to get their daily meds; it was very unsettling. I tend to put up what I see as a wall because I am highly sensitive, and the wall is my survival. Among all that traffic, CJ was sitting there very quietly with a familiar twinkle in his eye, pondering if he was going to get help.

The counselor finally comes out and tells us, "There are no beds available at this time; they are all filled." My heart stopped! I immediately thought, "What am I going to do now?" I remember CJ said nothing because it was as if I was his voice; it was always like that with us. The counselor continued by telling me "he would be fine going to his meetings and if he needed urgent help, you can call around to hospitals to see if they could get him a bed" As we drove home CJ was quiet, he did not want to be where he was and he did everything he could to stay clean but it was obvious he was going through withdrawals.

I made a few calls to different hospitals, but it seemed no one acknowledged me. It was perplexing and scary, and is still a problem to this day. I felt helpless, but I know I made every attempt to detox my son, and it was working. That's what makes this experience even harder, where, for a moment, like the peace within the eye of a storm, you feel you're getting through this.

"A moment before eternity"

The last two weeks before CJ's passing are an experience I shall hold closest to my heart until we meet again.

It was his supervisor at work in the catering business who suspected something was not right with him, and she suggested he take a few weeks off. I think that's when it hit CJ that he needed help and had hit rock bottom. He spent a lot of time in his room, and I know he didn't want to lose his job. We went to many meetings during this time at Seafield, OLPH, and Saint Joseph's, and I truly felt I had my son back.

In those precious borrowed days, we went for pizza, one of his favorites. He was outside with his skateboard and his girlfriend, Sam. He was playing basketball, he was just CJ again! Sitting down watching TV together, he would lean on me, giving me hugs as he often did, and he was happy again!

We went to Waldbaum's looking for his Charm lollipops, they were a little hard to find, and I remember after his death, when Waldbaum's closed, I cried

One eerie instance was on May 3rd in the afternoon. We were coming from Bellagio Pizza, his favorite. Funny, he didn't want to go in with me because he had no patience for waiting in a restaurant. On the way home, as we passed Saint Charles cemetery in Pine Lawn, a cemetery I always found peaceful looking, and of course, I like the name Charles, he suddenly turned to me and said, "Mom, I just had the most horrible feeling". He passed away on Tuesday, May 6th, just 3 days later. Charles is my son's first name, so after he passed, I thought about it and said to myself, *That's where you will be buried.* After all, he was raised catholic, it was like a message.

The night before he passed, he was out for a bit, and when he came home, I innocently asked, "Where were you?" He said he was just talking to a friend as he leaned on the banister of the stairs. I said "I love you more than life itself" as I had often told him, he said "I'm going to bed, Mom" with no sign that the burden he managed to get control of had returned, and what were to become his last words to me.

"What would you be doing now in your life…"

The funeral was pretty much a blur to me. All I can remember thinking and feeling is "How the hell did I walk away from CJ in that funeral hall?" I battled with that from the moment I left the funeral parlor, and the cemetery equally; it was agonizing.

My oldest brother, Jeffrey, recalls my last moments with CJ as he stood in the doorway of the empty room. Everyone left, I am leaning over his coffin, lightly tapping his chest and softly speaking to him. I put his favorite candies in his pocket, Smarties, Charm lollipops, and a note I had written to him. I am repeatedly kissing him. "Yes, no parent should ever have to bury their child."

When I look back at the events that transpired leading to his death, I see where I missed signs that should have told me there was something more than the difficulties of growing up going on here. For a time, I thought he was only struggling with Marijuana and pills.

I can find some comfort in knowing that CJ fought hard to rid himself of this demon of drug addiction. "Ultimately, he carried a ruthless burden with grace."

Shortly after he passed, his friends organized a concert in his memory. The amount of support and love I got sparked something in me. I found a way to survive, it brought me peace within a living hell otherwise. I felt compelled to carry on CJ's name and efforts to help others. This was the birth of The Beat Lives On, which came from his love for creating beats.

Our message and efforts would be my son's words to the world, and with every achievement, we honor CJ. To help those already addicted and to enlighten and embolden all others to turn their back on the perils of drugs at all costs.

To this day, I cannot speak to my husband about that day, and I know he went through more than I because he was up in his room much longer than I was. However, we can easily speak of what CJ was like, what he loved, and the funny moments in his short life. As for his brother, my younger son Raymond, there is silence. It may take many years of maturity before he puts into perspective his brother CJ's fate.

I sometimes get caught up in praying to the Virgin Mary to let me see my son for just three seconds, but I do feel I see and feel him in many ways throughout my days.

My heart is forever broken, but through his beautiful memories, I will survive and have dedicated myself to helping others. I have tremendous faith and peace that my CJ is busy in heaven helping those in need and me wherever he possibly can.

Ellyana DeLaTorre

By her mother, Eileen DeLaTorre

A Life of Love, Light, and Legacy

Ellyana DeLaTorre grew up on Long Island, NY, where her infectious laughter and radiant smile lit up every room she entered.

From an early age, Ellyana was a bright light to everyone around her. Her presence was magnetic, drawing people in with her warmth, good energy, and inspiring kindness. She was the kind of person who made others feel important, seen, and valued, even in momentary interactions.

As a young girl, Ellyana thrived in a loving home with her mom and dad. Four years after she was born, her younger brother, Jevani, arrived, solidifying her role as his protector, second mother, and biggest supporter. She adored her brother and vowed to always keep him safe, quickly coming to his defense when needed. While the siblings shared the typical bickering and competitions of childhood, their relationship was rooted in unconditional love and mutual respect.

Her parents were devoted to providing a nurturing and supportive environment, one that embraced both Ellyana and Jevani's individuality. They worked tirelessly to foster a home filled with love, understanding, and encouragement. Ellyana and Jevani's bond only grew

Ellyana DeLaTorre

stronger over the years, marked by countless moments of laughter, playful teasing, and deep connection.

One of the most influential relationships in Ellyana's life was with her grandmother, affectionately known as "Didi." Their connection transcended familial ties; they were confidants and close friends. Didi was a source of wisdom, strength, and unconditional support for Ellyana. Whether thrifting together, baking a new creation, binge-watching "Gilmore Girls," or simply enjoying each other's company, their moments together were precious and profoundly impactful on Ellyana's heart.

Ellyana's early years were filled with simple pleasures and creative pursuits. She excelled in gymnastics, dedicating herself to learning new routines and perfecting her form. Her love for competitive cheer was equally strong, as she thrived on the camaraderie and the thrill of performing. Her routines showcased a blend of grace and power, reflecting her spirited and determined personality. In addition to her athletic talents, Ellyana expressed herself through art and creativity.

She was a gifted artist who loved to draw, filling sketchbooks with imaginative creations. She also enjoyed creating YouTube videos, delighting her audience with what we now know as "Get Ready With Me" (GRWM) routines and shopping hauls. These videos highlighted her vibrant personality, creativity, and flair for connecting with others. Music was another cornerstone of her life. She sang along to her favorite songs with emotion and beauty, using music as both an outlet and a way to bond with the world around her. Her beloved dog, Charlie, was a constant companion who brought her immense joy. The two shared countless walks, cuddles, and adventures, further enriching her life with unconditional love and loyalty.

Friends were also a vital part of her world. Ellyana's warm and welcoming nature naturally drew people to her. She had a rare gift for forming deep connections and was always there for her friends with unwavering support and empathy. Whether helping someone in need or simply lending a shoulder to cry on, her kindness knew no bounds.

The Shadow of Struggles

While Ellyana's early years were filled with joy and enthusiasm, she also faced challenges that were often hidden behind her radiant smile. From a young age, she struggled with anxiety, a silent battle that became more complex as she grew older. Her anxiety evolved, eventually manifesting as obsessive-compulsive disorder (OCD). Simple tasks, like choosing an outfit or picking colors, often became overwhelming and stressful.

These challenges left her feeling frustrated and drained, but despite them, Ellyana focused on helping others. Supporting those around her provided her with strength and a distraction from the turmoil she often faced internally. As her parents, it was heartbreaking to witness her struggles and feel powerless to completely alleviate her pain.

When Ellyana was nine years old, her doctor confirmed what we had already suspected: she was showing signs of severe OCD. At the time, the diagnosis was met with a dismissive attitude, as the doctor assured us she would likely "grow out of it." Unfortunately, this lack of understanding about OCD's complexities left us without the immediate support we needed. OCD is a very real, isolating, and challenging condition, especially for a young child. Determined to support her, we sought treatments, researched extensively, and worked tirelessly to provide her with a nurturing environment. Together, we navigated therapy, medication, and coping mechanisms, forming a bond that strengthened as we faced each challenge together.

The Teenage Years: A Complex Journey

As Ellyana entered her teenage years, her world expanded with new experiences, relationships, and challenges. Her kindness and empathy made her a cherished friend, and her sense of humor brought joy to everyone around her.

Yet, her struggles with mental health grew more pronounced. At 17, Ellyana received a diagnosis of Autism Spectrum Disorder (ASD). Though the diagnosis was initially shocking, it provided clarity and explained much of what she had experienced throughout her life. Ellyana's case was a testament to what clinicians term "hiding in plain sight" or the "lost girls" phenomenon, where girls with autism are often diagnosed late due to their ability to mask symptoms. For Ellyana, this dual diagnosis of OCD and ASD meant navigating a complex and often overwhelming world. While the diagnosis brought answers, it also posed new challenges as she worked to find her place in a world that sometimes felt difficult to understand.

As a teenager, Ellyana faced the turbulent waters of adolescence. Her anxiety and OCD were compounded by the emotional challenges that many young adults face. Searching for solace, she sometimes experimented with outlets that offered temporary relief but came with lasting consequences. Unfortunately, this included involvement with the wrong crowds—groups that influenced her choices and left a lasting impact on her mental and emotional well-being.

Despite these struggles, Ellyana remained fiercely authentic. She embraced her individuality, channeling her energy into bold and creative self-expression. Her unique sense of style became a signature trait, a way of communicating her vibrant personality without saying a word. Music, too, remained a sanctuary. Through her favorite songs, she found solace, strength, and a voice for emotions she struggled to articulate.

Whether passionately singing along in the car or sharing playlists with friends, music connected her to the world and herself. By the time she turned 18, Ellyana's resilience and transformation were evident. She embraced every facet of who she was, flaws and struggles included. Her courage in the face of adversity became one of her defining qualities, inspiring those around her to live boldly and authentically.

A Tragic Loss and a Powerful Legacy

On the evening of August 4, 2021, Ellyana left her home with her best friend to watch the sunset. I still vividly remember her smile as she kissed me goodbye, the scent of her perfume, and the outfit she wore as she walked down the driveway. It was the last time we saw her. On August 5, 2021, Suffolk County Police and homicide detectives arrived at our home to deliver news that no parent should ever hear. Ellyana had passed away from fentanyl poisoning. The loss of our beautiful, vibrant daughter left an immeasurable void in the lives of all who loved her.

Ellyana is remembered as a truly remarkable person—someone whose love, care, and kindness touched everyone she met. She had an extraordinary ability to make people feel seen and valued, offering support in deeply personal and meaningful ways. Whether through a warm smile, a heartfelt conversation, or a simple act of kindness, Ellyana's empathy was genuine and transformative. Her humor and quick wit brought light even in difficult moments. She balanced kindness with laughter, making her the type of person people naturally gravitated toward. Her beauty, both inside and out, shone in everything she did. Ellyana's confidence inspired others to embrace their uniqueness, and her open heart and generous spirit made the world a better place.

Even in her absence, Ellyana's legacy of compassion and kindness continues to inspire. Stories of her thoughtful words and actions serve as powerful reminders of the impact one person can have. Her life, though tragically short, was filled with purpose and meaning.

Carrying Ellyana's Spirit Forward

In the wake of her passing, we channeled our grief into creating something meaningful. The Elly CARES Project was born to honor her memory and continue her mission of spreading kindness and raising awareness about mental health and substance abuse prevention.

The Elly CARES Project reflects Ellyana's values and spirit. Its mission is to provide support and safe spaces where individuals can feel heard and understood. One of the project's key initiatives is the Annual Ellyana DeLaTorre Stomp the Stigma 5K, a family-friendly community event that raises awareness about mental health challenges and honors Ellyana's life.

Another cornerstone of the project is the Ellyana DeLaTorre Memorial Scholarship, a $1,000 award given annually to a graduating student from Sequoya High School who has personally battled mental illness or supported a loved one through their struggles.

Applicants are asked to share their experiences in a short essay, reflecting on how they plan to use their journey to inspire and uplift others. The scholarship not only provides financial support but also validates the experiences of young people facing mental health challenges. It is a reminder that they are not alone and that their struggles do not define them.

A Legacy of Love and Kindness

Through the Elly CARES Project, Ellyana's light continues to touch lives. The organization partners with other mental health initiatives, attends mental health fairs, and creates programs that foster understanding and compassion. Ellyana's story is one of love, perseverance, and hope. Her legacy reminds us that even in the face of immense challenges, kindness and compassion have the power to make a lasting impact. Though her life was tragically short, her spirit endures through the lives she touched and the work carried out in her name.

Ellyana DeLaTorre will forever be remembered as a young woman who lived with joy, loved deeply, and inspired those around her to be their best selves. Her legacy is a beacon of hope for anyone navigating the complexities of mental health, proving that even in the darkest moments, love and light can prevail.

To learn more about Ellyana, please visit ellycaresproject.org.

———

The stories of **CJ Neuman, Ellyana DeLatorre, Michael Sena, and so many others taken too soon** are what drives this mission. We have a lot of work to do, and I intend to keep doing it.

As I move into the next section, I do so with gratitude for the people who have shared their stories, for those working toward change, and for the opportunity to be part of that effort.

25

GRATITUDE

I've always considered myself resilient, able to navigate challenges with grit and determination. But resilience doesn't mean being immune to struggle, and my journey has been full of twists and turns I never could have anticipated. It wasn't the path I envisioned growing up in a loving home with hardworking parents who instilled in me the values of kindness, integrity, and perseverance. Yet, every step of that journey led me to this moment, to this purpose, and for that, I am deeply grateful.

I never planned to be a teacher. As a kid, I dreamed of forecasting the weather, fascinated by its unpredictability and power. But life had other plans. Circumstances pushed me away from that path, leaving me adrift, unsure of my direction. Those were tough years, marked by a sense of failure and a gnawing question: *What now?* I took on menial jobs, questioning my choices and wondering if I had missed my chance to make something of myself.

It's funny how life has a way of redirecting us. Those jobs, seemingly insignificant at the time, taught me humility, patience, and the importance of showing up—even when it feels impossible. Without realizing it, I was preparing for something bigger. When teaching found me, I was hesitant, unsure if it was the right fit. But not soon after I stepped into the classroom, everything began to make sense.

Teaching was a calling. Every student who walked into my room brought their own story, their own struggles, and their own potential. My role was so much more than teaching, it was to help them discover who they were and who they could become. I didn't have all the answers, but I had a deep well of empathy, shaped by my challenges. And that made all the difference. For that, I am forever grateful.

Transforming Struggle into Purpose

Middle school had been a difficult time for me, marked by insecurity and social angst, augmented by the lies of a vicious rumor. Those experiences, though painful, shaped my approach as an educator. I understood the vulnerability of being young and the importance of creating a space where kids felt seen and valued. That is why I was adamant on spending the extra time with Finn, who needed to know he was important, and with PJ and Ryan, who needed an outlet to express their angst and frustrations. Some of the best conversations I ever had as an educator took place before school or during lunch periods with my students who needed a positive adult influence. It allowed me to learn the intricate and personal side of being a teacher. I learned as much from them as they did from me, all for simply letting these students know that they mattered.

Over the years, I met students who challenged me, inspired me, and taught me more than I ever could have taught them. Students like Finn, who battled social ostracism with courage; PJ, who showed me the transformative power of mentorship; and Parker, whose resilience in the face of physical and academic challenges was nothing short of extraordinary. Each of them reinforced a lesson I'd learned early on: you will be much more than their teacher.

These relationships shaped not only my teaching but also the programs I would later create through Long Island PREP. They showed me the importance of addressing the root causes of struggles—whether they stem from mental health, substance use, or external pressures—and the power of a united effort among students, parents, and educators. Every success story reminded me why this work matters and fueled my determination to do more. And for that, I am forever grateful.

My Gift of My Struggle

Ironically, it was my struggles that gave me the perspective I needed to truly connect with my students and their families. Anxiety, once a silent shadow in my life, forced me to confront my vulnerability. Seeking help was one of the hardest things I've ever done, but it was also the most transformative. Therapy taught me that asking for help isn't a weakness—it's a strength. That realization became a cornerstone of my work with Long Island PREP.

When I see a student struggling, I recognize pieces of myself in their fear and uncertainty. I know the courage it takes to ask for help, and I work to ensure they feel safe enough to do so. My battle with anxiety became a lens through which I view the world—a reminder that we all carry invisible burdens and that kindness and understanding can make all the difference.

A New Approach for a New Generation

Long Island PREP grew out of these experiences and the lessons I've learned along the way. It's a testament to the coalescence of experience and ideas; it's a philosophy rooted in empathy and action. The failures of the past—scare tactics, stigma, and superficial solutions—showed me what *not* to do. Instead, Long Island PREP focuses on prevention, education, and collaboration. It's about giving kids the tools to navigate life's challenges and creating a support system that surrounds them with care and understanding.

Gratitude in Action

Today, I look back on my journey with gratitude—not because it was easy, but because it shaped me into the person I am. Every failure, every setback, every sleepless night taught me something valuable. They prepared me to meet my students where they are, to see their struggles through a compassionate lens, and to guide them toward a brighter future.

I am grateful for my parents, who gave me the foundation of love and support that I now strive to provide for others. I am grateful for my students, who remind me every day why this work matters. And I am grateful for the challenges that have tested me, for they have become the fuel for my purpose.

Paying it Forward

Long Island PREP is so much more than addressing problems—it's about creating solutions that last. It's about empowering kids to see their worth, helping families navigate the complexities of parenting, and fostering a sense of community that uplifts everyone involved. It's a mission born from struggle, shaped by experience, and driven by an unwavering belief in the potential of my work. Teaching has given me a perspective on life that I am unsure would have been so clear in any other profession. That is why I have devoted the scope of my experience to bridging the gap between today and the generations of tomorrow. For all this has given me, it is the least I can do.

For all of this, despite never wanting to be a teacher, I am forever grateful.

As I reflect on my journey of creating Long Island PREP, numerous forces converged to make it possible. I knew I could use my life experiences and educational background to make a difference. But there was something I knew I would need help with. The caveats to an education program have their roots in the classroom, with students and the everyday flow of teaching and learning. I had that covered. However, the administration of academic concepts, research, and best practices would have to come together with the knowledge and experience of a professional in the field of education at a higher level.

Enter Dr. Anne Rullan. "Doc," as I've come to refer to her, puts it beautifully when she reveals her thoughts about our first-ever conversation regarding her involvement in Long Island PREP.

"It was so out of the blue. There was a voicemail on my phone, and when I heard 'Hi Dr. Rullan, this is Paul Vecchione. I would like to

speak with you about something at your earliest convenience. I immediately thought, What *hell could he possibly want from me?"*

It's true. Usually, there were very few reasons why I would reach out
to Dr. Rullan. Before she retired, she was the Assistant Superintendent
for Curriculum and Instruction in the district where I was teaching. In
the four years we worked simultaneously in the district, we interacted
three times. Our path rarely required passing. A few factors worked in
my favor that may have compelled Dr. Rullan to help with Long Island
PREP. She is very smart, organized, recently retired, and still active in
the academic community. So I gave it a shot. When Anne called me
back, I gave her the full run-down of what I was doing and looking for.
I needed someone to help with the Prep For Life curriculum and
research for the programs. Someone who knew the ins and outs of
curriculum writing and the education administration world. And, she
was it.

"That sounds great, I am in!" I remember her saying.

Dr. Rullan not only accepted my invitation to participate in the monumental task, but she has also been a staple in its development, evolu-
tion, and application. When it came time to inquire about a blurb for
the book, she didn't hesitate, and the familiar "I'm in!" was uttered
again.

26

ANNE'S STORY

I have not been a stranger to understanding the need for a healthy mental mind. One that can cope, that can rely on stress management strategies, and work hard not to let those overwhelming moments take over their behavior and decisions. Experiencing the death of my father at 18 may have been the beginning of really understanding how important my mental well-being was, but a true realization started with the birth of my son. His prognosis was not good - if he survived birth, maybe five minutes, five months, but certainly not a year. Even writing this down, at this very moment, the emotions, the pain, and the grief sweep back over me.

My son was diagnosed with congenital kidney disease. As he was in utero, several other issues became part of the problem. My husband and I went from one doctor to another, and I was closely monitored throughout the pregnancy. We were determined that we would have a good outcome. I researched as much as I could about his developmental delays, had a team ready for his birth as we thought he might need immediate surgery, and I started the practice of controlled breathing. It was my experience at the time that a doctor would tell you exactly what they thought you could handle at the time. I wanted all the information. I wanted to be able to do something. I wanted my child to live.

I was induced early as the latest scan showed him to be in distress. They indicated that he would be ventilated until he could breathe on his own. Luckily, he just needed oxygen. Off he went into the neonatal intensive care unit, and so his journey began. In the first two years of his life, he underwent nine hospital procedures. He lost one kidney due to it being polycystic and the other had a Ureteropelvic Junction (UPJ) Obstruction. a congenital heart defect, where a baby is born with an abnormal opening between the chambers of the heart, usually called a "ventricular septal defect" (VSD), meaning there's a hole between the two lower chambers of the heart; found his appendix needed to be removed; "A floating appendix" refers to a medical condition where the appendix, a small organ attached to the large intestine, is not firmly attached to the surrounding tissue and appears to be "floating" freely within the abdominal cavity, which in turn, caused an Intussusception: a condition where one part of the intestine telescopes into another, causing an obstruction. Alongside that, he was diagnosed with Duane's Syndrome, a rare congenital eye disorder characterized by an inability to fully move the affected eye outward (abduction). It is caused by an abnormality in the nerves that control eye movement. Just for good measure, he needed a tonsillectomy and had his adenoids removed.

At the time, I was in a Master's Program getting my M.S. in Elementary Education. I soaked up what I learned about child development and questioned those in education about how children who have had an intensive medical history perform in school, socially, mentally, emotionally, and academically. One of my professors said that he always found that children who have been diagnosed with some type of disease usually seem so well-adjusted in school. From his perspective, these children have endured more in their lives from birth to being school-age than most people do in their lifetimes. That perspective resonated with me.

There were other bumps in the road, he contracted a cholesteatoma, a cyst-like growth that develops in the middle ear, behind the eardrum.

In his case, the mass was already pressing into the brain. They had no choice but to remove it with surgery.

I was teaching first grade, and I always felt that one of my main goals as an educator was to provide children with the love of learning. With the love of learning came the understanding that we need to take risks, ask questions, test out our ideas, and reflect on the processes of failure for learning so we eventually have success. As I moved to teaching fifth graders, I realized that without social, emotional, and mental well-being, students would not thrive. Already in fifth grade, students were conscious about "not knowing things," forgetting why they were in school. I recall reminding students that they were in school to learn new things, ask questions, and take that information to formulate their thoughts. There began the journey to having students ask themselves:

"Who am I as a learner? A reader? A writer? A mathematician? A scientist? A historian?" etc.

"What do I already know?"

"What do I need to learn?"

"What do I want to learn?"

"How will I learn new things?

Answering the above questions relies on student metacognition and reflection. As I learned later, these strategies are equally important, if not more, for a healthy mental well-being.

I moved on into administration, first as an elementary building principal and then moved into the central office, eventually becoming an assistant superintendent for curriculum and instruction. Although not in my title, I was also responsible for instructional personnel. In all positions, the value of establishing meaningful relationships with students, parents, community members, and educational colleagues was paramount.

In the role of working as a district administrator, I could see the full K-12 perspective of providing students the tools and strategies necessary to be successful after leaving our doors. One glaring fact stood in the way of making that happen. How do we support students and their families with the skills of being healthy, mentally, emotionally, and physically? How do we have them take responsibility for their learning? How do we support independent and reflective thinkers? How do we support creativity, innovation, and transformation? These indicators should not be left to chance. Education needs to have a platform for a systematic approach to providing our students, our future, with the tools they need to be successful.

So, where to begin? Before I retired, the district I worked in looked at programs that supported mindfulness, drug awareness, and health curricula that included mental health. All the programs had something to offer, but not everything that needed to be offered. So we took pieces from each one and put together something that we believed worked for our students. Regardless, they were heavily geared to elementary students, and none supported students who were in crisis. We saw, just like other districts, an uptick in school phobia, anxiety, drug use, and behaviors. We started taking a look at these issues by using a Response to Intervention (RtI) or Multi-tiered Systems of Support (MTSS) approach. This led us to realize that we were missing large pieces in a core curriculum, targeted interventions, and data collection to inform future decision-making. It was time to make a change.

But as I mentioned, I was retiring and planned on consulting in education. Then the pandemic came and changed everything about how we provide an education that meets the needs of the whole child for all children. I began consulting at that time, first on how to deliver quality instruction in a virtual and/or digital hybrid environment and how to create a community in the same situation. Effective assessment practices in a hybrid learning environment, creating a classroom community, etc. I love what I do and love that I am engaged in the education process and am committed to being a lifelong learner.

One day, totally out of the blue, a teacher, Paul, reached out to me from the district I retired from. Not knowing what to expect as we were mere acquaintances, he shared with me his dream and passion for developing a multi-faceted approach to ultimately have students build the skills necessary to resist illicit drugs and substances. His enthusiasm was contagious, but I wondered why he thought of me. He shared that he needed someone to write a curriculum. He outlined his research, having a dedicated curriculum that embeds a multitude of strategies and skills for students, a program that specifically supports students at-risk, professional development for educators, parents/guardians, and community members.

I was, of course, immediately interested, but wanted to make sure that my decision to become part of this project was based on research, best practices, and accessibility for educators to implement. What I found was that research indicates that a comprehensive mental wellness program incorporating community outreach, professional development, and a Multi-Tiered System of Support (MTSS) approach can be highly effective in preventing and reducing student drug and substance abuse, with studies showing positive outcomes when targeting different tiers of student needs with tailored interventions, including education, social-emotional learning, and access to counseling services when necessary.

Using a well-structured MTSS system allows for early identification of at-risk students, providing universal prevention strategies for all students (Tier 1), targeted interventions for students showing early signs of substance use (Tier 2), and intensive support for students with established substance abuse issues (Tier 3). Additionally, engaging parents, community leaders, and local organizations through outreach initiatives can significantly strengthen prevention efforts by creating a supportive environment and promoting positive norms around substance use. Equipping school staff with comprehensive training on substance abuse prevention, mental health awareness, and effective intervention strategies is crucial for the successful implementation of an MTSS approach. Incorporating SEL programs within an MTSS framework can build resilience, coping skills, and positive decision-making abilities, which can serve as protective factors against substance abuse.

Paul provided an outline with a focus on personal development through the topics of wellness, self-esteem/confidence, and individuality. Topics that explore interpersonal skills are meaningful relationships, expressive communication, and stress management, and to address substance abuse prevention, lessons focused on coping skills, illicit substance awareness, decision-making, and goal setting.

Paul and I discussed the importance of designing lessons that provide engaging activities to promote active learning and participation across all grade levels, and designing a program that fosters personal growth and positive decision-making skills, as well as the utilization of modern educational tools to enhance student involvement and learning outcomes. Along with the content, lessons need to integrate character-building themes and the Prevention & Resilience Enrichment Program's Cornerstone Ideology of peer pressure resistance; navigating misinformation, exposure awareness, and the importance of parent involvement.

The first task was to research operational definitions of all that was above. After careful consideration, the curriculum was designed to move horizontally, building upon and strategically revisiting prior learning to consolidate into new learning. Additionally, each prior year's lessons provided the foundation for the vertical alignment, once again strategically revisiting prior learning to make meaning of new learning.

At this point, I was charged about this opportunity to help design not only the curriculum, but also the resources of strategies to use for students potentially at-risk. Little did I know at the time how fortuitous it was for me to have been able to access a better understanding of how a healthy mental outlook is essential in dealing with the most unsettling and stressful situations. If I wasn't already invested in how important a comprehensive approach to providing students and their families with the tools necessary to navigate the unknown, a phone call from my son telling me he had an MRI and he just received a phone call telling him to drive to the nearest hospital. My son had a mass in the brain that was impeding his ability to complete daily functions.

Surgery was the only option, but due to the location of the tumor, the risks included mobility and eating issues, and death. There was no choice, surgery was his only option. Afterwards, his recovery went well, but we got the news of his diagnosis of the tumor being a medulloblastoma, which is a cancerous brain tumor that starts in the cerebellum, near the brainstem. The good news is that they think they got it all out; the bad news is that it spread throughout his spine and down his legs.

I immediately felt as if my world had turned upside down. No amount of preparation could have readied me for the emotional rollercoaster that came with navigating his treatment, hospital visits, and the uncertainties that lay ahead. Fear, anxiety, and sadness threatened to consume me, but I knew I had to find ways to stay strong for him and myself. Journaling, practicing positive affirmations, and embracing gratitude became my lifelines, helping me find balance and resilience in the face of unimaginable challenges.

Writing became my emotional release. I would pour my thoughts onto paper—every fear, frustration, and fleeting moment of hope. Journaling allowed me to process my emotions rather than letting them fester inside. On days when the weight of uncertainty felt unbearable, I could reflect on my words and recognize the strength I was cultivating.

Beyond being a coping mechanism, journaling also became a tool for clarity. When faced with difficult decisions, writing down my thoughts helped me untangle the complexity of my emotions and find a sense of direction. It reminded me that despite the overwhelming situation, I could process and navigate it one step at a time.

There were days when I felt completely drained, emotionally and physically. On those days, my inner dialogue could have easily been filled with despair. Instead, I turned to positive affirmations. Every morning, I would be by my son's side and promise him we would be together and that he was strong, he was going to make it. For myself, I had a small notebook in which I wrote the following:

"I am strong enough to get through this."

"I have the patience and courage to support my son."

"We will find joy even on the hardest days."

At first, I felt it was a meaningless exercise, but over time, these affirmations rewired my thoughts. They became my armor against the doubt and fear that tried to creep in. Speaking these words aloud helped me cultivate a mindset of resilience and hope, which, in turn, allowed me to be a pillar of strength for my son.

And if the medulloblastoma diagnosis wasn't enough, we were later faced with another unexpected finding—my son's genetic testing results showed that he had 17q12 Deletion Syndrome. This meant he had a deletion on the 17th chromosome, a condition linked to kidney, pancreatic, eye, and ear issues. It wasn't inherited from us, and as far as doctors knew, it wasn't connected to his brain tumor or cancer. However, it did explain why his case was so complicated and why treatment had to be adjusted continuously.

During hospital stays, difficult treatments, and long nights filled with worry, it would have been easy to focus only on the hardship. But I made a conscious effort to practice gratitude. Every morning, I would write down at least three things I was grateful for, no matter how small. Some days, it was the kindness of a nurse, a moment of laughter with my son, or simply the warmth of the sun on my face.

Gratitude didn't erase the pain, but it shifted my focus. It reminded me that even in the darkest times, light still existed. It strengthened my ability to endure, showing me that love and hope were always present, even when life felt overwhelming.

Through journaling, affirmations, and gratitude, I found a way to keep moving forward. These practices didn't change my son's diagnosis or the new genetic discovery, but they transformed the way I faced them —with strength, grace, and an unwavering belief in hope. This sense of strength, grace, and hope - I want that for everyone. I want to share mental health strategies that enhance emotional resilience, reduce stress, improve focus, strengthen relationships, and boost overall well-being, leading to better decision-making, increased productivity, and a more balanced, fulfilling life for everyone.

All of these experiences, along with the promising efforts of Paul Vecchione and Long Island PREP, is why I took the leap and decided to join the movement it is creating.

27

MY CHALLENGE TO YOU

As you turn this final page, in true teacher fashion, I want to leave you with the opportunity for growth—a challenge to look inward, reflect on your experiences, and transform the lessons you've learned into a force for good. You've read my story, and while you're probably ready to close this final chapter, I hope it inspires you to write your own as you forge your journey forward.

The path to understanding is rarely straightforward. It wasn't for me, and it likely isn't for you. But here's the thing: it's never too late to turn experience into action. Each of us carries a unique story—one filled with struggles, triumphs, and lessons. And within those stories lies the potential to inspire change, offer hope, and create ripples of positivity that extend far beyond ourselves. The question is, will you use it?

We're living in a time when division and discord seem to dominate the narrative. It's easy to get caught up in the noise, to feel helpless or overwhelmed by the challenges around us. But I truly believe that the antidote isn't found in blame or judgment—it's found in connection, empathy, and purposeful action. And it starts with us.

It starts with choosing to be a light source in someone else's life. To listen more and judge less. To empathize with a point of view that may not be ours. To take the lessons we've learned—whether from our failures or our victories—and use them to lift others. It's not about being perfect; it's about being present, intentional, and willing to grow.

So, here's my challenge to you: Reflect on your story and ask yourself:

- What have your experiences taught you?
- Are there gaps that need to be filled, and will you have the humility to seek what you need to fill them?
- Will you use your experiences to make a difference, not just in your own life, but in the lives of others?
- Will you show up for your community, your family, and yourself with kindness, courage, and purpose?
- Will you embrace the idea that even small actions matter?

Pick up a pen and journal about it. You may be surprised at the power of expressive communication and its ability to spur action.

We hold the keys to a better world for our children and future generations. But creating that world requires us to take a hard look at ourselves, to own our stories, and to use them as fuel for change. It demands compassion, resolve, and the courage to show up—not just for ourselves, but for one another. It won't always be easy, but the most meaningful journeys rarely are. If there's one thing I've learned, the challenges we face can shape us into stronger, more compassionate people if we let them. And those lessons, when shared, have the power to transform not just individuals but entire communities.

The power to make a difference is in your hands. Are you up for the challenge?

I never wanted to be a teacher, but my perceived road not taken, for me, made all the difference. Will yours?

28

OUR IMPACT

S ome say teaching is a thankless profession, or that educators will never truly know the impact they've had on their students. I believe this to be true, but I couldn't be prouder of Long Island PREP. The stories you've just read—the students I've worked with, the lives I've impacted—are a testament to the mission that drives me daily. This is about what we can do together.

Now that you've picked up this book, you can see how I've helped these children and their families. And more importantly, you'll see how we all can continue to make a difference—one student at a time.

PREP National

What began as a local initiative—Long Island PREP—has grown into a national movement. With a mission rooted in education, prevention, and intervention, Long Island PREP made a lasting impact on schools and communities by addressing the critical issues of substance abuse and mental health. As the demand for these programs grew beyond New York, so did the vision.

PREP National was born from that expansion, bringing the same evidence-based programs, crisis intervention strategies, and educational resources to schools, prisons, and community organizations around the world. What started as a regional effort has evolved into an extensive commitment to protecting and empowering the next generation.

www.prepinternational.com

Testimonials

Students, North Babylon School District, North Babylon, New York

"The coping skills activity helped me remember what healthy coping mechanisms are and what I usually do as a little reminder to practice my good coping skills. This helped me out a little throughout the past couple of weeks. continuing to meditate , thinking before speaking , mindfulness , etc."

— ALYSSA J. 12TH GRADE

" I learned the true dangers of the opioid crisis and who was behind it. Coping skills activity opened my eyes and showed me the importance of finding other ways of coping with stress."

— -ALI B. 11TH GRADE

"The R.I.C.A.P.P program is very effective and will prepare middle school kids for their high school years!"

"I learned that journaling helps you realize things you have done and not done, and if you fail multiple times, you become stronger!"

— TANIYA B. 12TH GRADE

" I liked the meaningful relationships and coping skills activities the best!"

" The R.I.C.A.P.P program is good for middle school kids, and it will help them to get the young adult experience before high school."

— ARIELLE 12TH GRADE

 " These programs helped me in my personal life, especially coping skills and self-esteem, and I use the journaling activity on a regular basis now."

— A. JONES 12TH GRADE

Ask yourself: Do any of these stories remind you of yourself?

Administrator, Center Moriches School District, Center Moriches, New York

 " I have seen some incredible results when using it as an intervention resource with students who have struggled with substance issues and wanted to be involved in cessation groups to give them the tools to make better choices. "

"Long Island PREP has been an amazing resource in both a classroom setting and an administrative setting. I have seen some incredible results when using it as an intervention resource with students who have struggled with substance issues and wanted to be involved in cessation groups to give them the tools to make better choices. In a classroom setting, I was able to implement LI PREP as a preventative measure by educating and building self-awareness, setting goals, and building confidence in students."

— KATY FORMAN - ASSISTANT HIGH SCHOOL

PRINCIPAL, CENTER MORICHES SCHOOL DISTRICT,
CENTER MORICHES, NEW YORK

"To tackle the mental health crisis our students face requires new and innovative ways of thinking. Long Island PREP has created a system that addresses the core issue of substance abuse in children and young adults. They aren't just scratching the surface. It is a deeper systems approach that aims to make students' mental health and wellness an absolute priority, all while offering an effective partnership model for schools."

— DR.WILLIAM BRENNAN,ED.D. SUPERINTENDENT,
MASSAPEQUA UNION FREE SCHOOL DISTRICT,
MASSAPEQUA, NEW YORK

"Early education that stresses prevention and highlights the danger of drug use is an important tool in our fight against substance abuse on Long Island. I applaud Long Island PREP for their willingness to engage our youth in the community and look forward to seeing it succeed in the years to come."

— STEVE BELLONE, FORMER SUFFOLK COUNTY
EXECUTIVE, SUFFOLK COUNTY, NEW YORK

LONG ISLAND
P.R.E.P
Prevention and Resilience Enrichment Program

(Click Link or Scan QR Code)

What is LI Prep (link)	**RICAPP** (link)	**Prep For Life** (link)

Knowledge Is Power (link)	**Our Portal** (link)	**Prep Academy** (link)

RICAPP

Expanding RICAPP into Clinical Settings

Originally developed to support schools in managing student mental health and crisis intervention, RICAPP has quickly proven its value and necessity beyond the educational setting. Mental health professionals in clinical environments face similar challenges: no centralized system to manage crises, track interventions, or maintain consistent communication with families. This gap leads to fragmented care, slower response times, and missed opportunities to support clients effectively.

Recognizing this need, **RICAPP Therapeutic** was launched to bring the same powerful, structured approach to therapists and clinical practices. As a cloud-based SaaS platform, RICAPP Therapeutic empowers mental health professionals with real-time tools to document and manage client crises, track progress, and engage families in the treatment process.

By expanding into the broader mental health community, RICAPP is now helping to improve client outcomes, enhance continuity of care, and reduce provider burnout—delivering a much-needed solution to a long-standing problem in therapeutic care.

Qualitative Study Dec 2024-March 2025

Live Participant Study Performed By:

Christina DiBernardo, LMHC, MSED, ACS
Executive Director and Founder , *Expressive Connections Mental Health Counseling* **ExpressiveConnectionsMHC.com**

Beta Testing Summary: RICAPP - Youth Mental Wellness Program

Program Overview

A three-month beta testing phase was conducted for a new program designed to promote mental and emotional wellness in children, teens, and young adults. The program focused on addressing symptoms of anxiety, depression, and executive dysfunction through targeted interventions and coping strategies. A total of 12 participants, ranging from 11 to 22 years old, completed the 3-month beta test program.

Key Outcomes

The program demonstrated significant positive outcomes across multiple domains:

- **Symptom Reduction**: 83% of participants and/or their parents reported a significant reduction in unwanted symptoms and behaviors within the three-month trial period.
- **Coping Skills Development**: Participants demonstrated a 45% increase in knowledge of effective coping skills as reported by themselves or their parents.

- **Strategy Effectiveness**: 75% of participants reported finding the learned coping strategies to be effective 75% of the time, with effectiveness varying based on specific situations.

Areas of Progress

Participants reported notable improvements in the following areas:

1. **Stress Management**: Significant reduction in overall stress levels and improved ability to recognize stress triggers.
2. **Resilience**: Enhanced ability to cope with challenges and setbacks.
3. **Life Skills Development**: Improvements in practical skills such as organization, time management, and task completion.
4. **Communication**: Increased openness with parents and support networks regarding mental health challenges.

Coping Strategies Implemented

The program utilized a variety of evidence-based coping strategies tailored to address specific symptom clusters:

For Anxiety

- **Mindfulness Practices**: Daily guided meditation and breathing exercises
- **Cognitive Restructuring**: Identifying and challenging catastrophic thinking patterns
- **Gradual Exposure**: A Systematic Approach to Facing Fears
- **Somatic Regulation**: Progressive muscle relaxation and body scanning techniques
- **Worry Scheduling**: Designated "worry time" to contain excessive rumination

For Depression

- **Behavioral Activation**: Scheduled engagement in pleasurable and mastery activities
- **Gratitude Practices**: Daily journaling focused on positive experiences
- **Social Connection**: Structured activities to maintain support networks
- **Physical Activity**: Regular movement incorporated into daily routines
- **Sleep Hygiene**: Establishment of consistent sleep schedules and pre-sleep routines

For Executive Dysfunction

- **Task Breakdown**: Breaking complex assignments into manageable steps
- **Visual Organization Systems**: Color-coded calendars and reminder systems
- **Time Management Techniques**: Pomodoro method and time blocking
- **Environmental Modifications**: Creating dedicated, distraction-reduced workspaces
- **Routine Development**: Establishing consistent daily patterns for essential activities

- **Self-Monitoring Tools**: Digital and analog tracking systems for task completion

Observed Impact on Adolescent Accountability

Clinical staff observed a notable increase in accountability among participants aged 14-22 when using this program compared to traditional therapy approaches. Key observations included:

- **Enhanced Task Completion:** Adolescents demonstrated higher rates of following through on assigned therapeutic activities and homework.
- **Increased Strategy Implementation:** Teens were significantly more likely to attempt and consistently apply learned coping strategies when they knew their progress was being tracked within the program.
- **Engagement with Documentation:** The program's structured tracking elements created a positive accountability framework that resonated particularly well with the adolescent population.
- **Measurable Progress Motivation:** Participants reported that viewing their tracked progress within the program provided tangible evidence of their efforts and motivated continued engagement.

This improved accountability represents a significant advantage over standard clinical documentation methods, which are typically not visible to clients and therefore do not provide the same motivational benefits.

ENDNOTES

10. The Devastating Facts

1. https://www.cdc.gov/mmwr/volumes/73/su/su7304a9.htm
2. Health Resources and Services Administration (HRSA). 2024. "Health Workforce Shortage Areas." U.S. Department of Health and Human Services. Accessed April 4, 2025 https://data.hrsa.gov/ ; https://www.ruralhealthinfo.org/topics/mental-health
3. National Institute of Mental Health (NIMH). 2023. "Mental Illness." *National Institutes of Health.* Accessed April 4, 2025. https://www.nimh.nih.gov/
4. Centers for Disease Control and Prevention. (2023). *Youth Risk Behavior Survey Data Summary & Trends Report: 2011–2021.* U.S. Department of Health and Human Services.https://www.cdc.gov/healthyyouth/data/yrbs/pdf/YRBS_Data-Summary-Trends_Report2023_508.pdf
5. Ranji, U., Frederiksen, B., & Salganicoff, A. (2023). *Anxiety and depression in women: A growing crisis.* The Commonwealth Fund. https://www.commonwealth-fund.org/publications
6. Centers for Disease Control and Prevention. (2023). *Youth Risk Behavior Survey Data Summary & Trends Report: 2011–2021.* U.S. Department of Health and Human Services. https://www.cdc.gov/healthyyouth/data/yrbs/pdf/YRBS_Data-Summary-Trends_Report2023_508.pdf
7. Centers for Disease Control and Prevention. (2022). *Mental health, suicidality, and connectedness among high school students during the COVID-19 pandemic — Adolescent Behaviors and Experiences Survey, United States, January–June 2021. MMWR Supplements, 71*(Suppl–3), 16–21.;
   https://wonder.cdc.gov/ ;
   https://www.cdc.gov/mmwr/volumes/69/wr/mm6945a3.htm ; https://www.cdc.gov/mmwr/volumes/70/wr/mm7024e1.htm;
   https://jamanetwork.com/journals/jamanetworkopen/fullarticle/2780135 ;
   https://www.cdc.gov/mmwr/volumes/71/su/su7103a3.htm
8. National Institute of Mental Health. (2023). *Major depression among adolescents.* U.S. Department of Health and Human Services. https://www.nimh.nih.gov/health/statistics/major-depression#part_2551
9. Centers for Disease Control and Prevention. (2023). *Data and statistics on children's mental health.* https://www.cdc.gov/childrensmentalhealth/data.html; Health Resources and Services Administration. (2022). *National Survey of Children's Health: Mental and Behavioral Health, 2016–2020.* Available at: https://mchb.hrsa.gov/sites/default/files/mchb/data-research/nsch-mental-health-factsheet.pdf;
   Meng, J. F., & Wiznitzer, E. (2024). Factors associated with not receiving mental health services among children with a mental disorder in early childhood in the United States, 2021–2022. *Preventing Chronic Disease, 21,* 240126. http://dx.doi.org/10.5888/pcd21.240126
10. Centers for Disease Control and Prevention. (2022). Mental health, suicidality, and connectedness among high school students during the COVID-19 pandemic —

Adolescent Behaviors and Experiences Survey, United States, January–June 2021. *MMWR Supplements, 71*(Suppl-3), 16–21. https://www.cdc.gov/mmwr/volumes/71/su/su7103a3.htm ; Health Resources and Services Administration. (2022). *National Survey of Children's Health: Mental and behavioral health, 2016–2020.* https://mchb.hrsa.gov/sites/default/files/mchb/data-research/nsch-mental-health-factsheet.pdf ; Santomauro, D. F., et al. (2021). Global prevalence and burden of depressive and anxiety disorders in 204 countries and territories in 2020 due to the COVID-19 pandemic. *The Lancet, 398*(10312), 1700–1712. https://www.thelancet.com/journals/lancet/article/PIIS0140-6736(21)02143-7/fulltext

11. Centers for Disease Control and Prevention. (2023). *Youth Risk Behavior Survey data summary & trends report: 2011–2021.* https://www.cdc.gov/healthyyouth/data/yrbs/pdf/YRBS_Data-Summary-Trends_Report2023_508.pdf ; Education Week. (2023). Why America has a youth mental health crisis, and how schools can help. https://www.edweek.org/leadership/why-america-has-a-youth-mental-health-crisis-and-how-schools-can-help/2023/10 ; National Center for Education Statistics. (2022). *School Pulse Panel: Mental health and well-being.* https://nces.ed.gov/schoolsurvey/spp/ ; Urban Institute. (2022). *The pandemic's impact on children's mental health and academic performance.* https://www.urban.org/research/publication/pandemics-impact-childrens-mental-health-and-academic-performance

12. Greenberg, P. E., Fournier, A.-A., Simes, M., Berman, R., & Koenigsberg, S. H. (2021). The economic burden of adults with major depressive disorder in the United States (2010 and 2018). *Pharmacoeconomics, 39*(5), 653–665. https://doi.org/10.1007/s40273-021-01019-4 ;

    Gallup. (2022). *The economic cost of poor employee mental health.* https://www.gallup.com/workplace/404978/economic-cost-poor-employee-mental-health.aspx ; World Health Organization. (2022). *Mental health at work.* https://www.who.int/news-room/fact-sheets/detail/mental-health-at-work ; Mental Health America. (2013). *Depression in the workplace.* https://www.mhanational.org/depression-workplace

13. Health Resources and Services Administration. (2024). *Designated Health Professional Shortage Areas statistics.* https://data.hrsa.gov/tools/shortage-area/hpsa-find; AAMC Research and Action Institute. (2022). *Exploring barriers to mental health care in the U.S.* https://www.aamcresearchinstitute.org/our-work/issue-brief/exploring-barriers-mental-health-care-us; Deloitte Health Equity Institute. (2024). *The projected costs and economic impact of mental health inequities in the United States.* https://www2.deloitte.com/us/en/pages/life-sciences-and-health-care/articles/projected-costs-of-mental-health-inequities.html

14. National Academy of Medicine. (2019). *Taking action against clinician burnout.* https://nam.edu/systematic-review-clinician-burnout/; Mayo Clinic Proceedings. (2023). Changes in burnout and satisfaction with work-life integration in physicians during the first 2 years of the COVID-19 pandemic. *Mayo Clinic Proceedings.* https://www.mayoclinicproceedings.org/article/S0025-6196(22)00543-8/fulltext; Education Week. (2023). Why America has a youth mental health crisis, and how schools can help. https://www.edweek.org/leadership/why-america-has-a-youth-mental-health-crisis-and-how-schools-can-help/2023/10; American Psychological Association. (2021). *Stress in America: Law enforcement.* https://www.apa.org/news/press/releases/stress; U.S. Surgeon General. (2022). *Framework for workplace mental health and well-being.* https://www.hhs.gov/surgeongeneral/priorities/workplace-well-being/index.html

15. Boers, E., Afzali, M. H., Newton, N. C., & Conrod, P. J. (2019). Association of screen time and depression in adolescence. *JAMA Pediatrics, 173*(9), 853–859. https://jamanetwork.com/journals/jamapediatrics/fullarticle/2737909; Twenge, J. M., Joiner, T. E., Rogers, M. L., & Martin, G. N. (2017). Increases in depressive symptoms, suicide-related outcomes, and suicide rates among U.S. adolescents after 2010 and links to increased new media screen time. *Clinical Psychological Science, 6*(1), 3–17. https://doi.org/10.1177/2167702617723376; Centers for Disease Control and Prevention. (2023). *Youth Risk Behavior Survey data summary & trends report: 2011–2021.* https://www.cdc.gov/healthyyouth/data/yrbs/pdf/YRBS_Data-Summary-Trends_Report2023_508.pdf

16. Centers for Disease Control and Prevention. (2023). *Youth Risk Behavior Survey data summary & trends report: 2011–2021.* https://www.cdc.gov/healthyyouth/data/yrbs/pdf/YRBS_Data-Summary-Trends_Report2023_508.pdf; Hamm, M. P., Newton, A. S., Chisholm, A., Shulhan, J., Milne, A., Sundar, P., ... & Hartling, L. (2018). Prevalence and effect of cyberbullying on children and young people: A scoping review of social media studies. *JAMA Pediatrics, 172*(8), 772–780. https://jamanetwork.com/journals/jamapediatrics/fullarticle/2686048; John, A., Glendenning, A. C., Marchant, A., Montgomery, P., Stewart, A., Wood, S., ... & Hawton, K. (2020). The impact of cyberbullying on mental health outcomes in adolescents. *The Lancet Child & Adolescent Health, 4*(8), 611–622. https://www.thelancet.com/journals/lanchi/article/PIIS2352-4642(20)30165-8/fulltext; National Institute of Mental Health. (2023). *Suicide risk factors.* https://www.nimh.nih.gov/health/topics/suicide-prevention#part_153173

17. Fardouly, J., Pinkus, R. T., & Vartanian, L. R. (2021). Social media and body image concerns: Further considerations of potential positive impacts. *Body Image, 39,* 137–147. https://doi.org/10.1016/j.bodyim.2021.07.005; American Psychological Association. (2023). *Health advisory on social media use in adolescence.* https://www.apa.org/topics/social-media-internet/health-advisory-adolescent-social-media-use; Saunders, J. F., Eaton, A. A., & Van Diest, A. M. (2022). Social media use and disordered eating in young adolescents. *Journal of Adolescent Health, 70*(4), 652–658. https://doi.org/10.1016/j.jadohealth.2021.11.015; Wilksch, S. M., O'Shea, A., Ho, P., Byrne, S., & Wade, T. D. (2019). Social media use and the risk of eating disorders in adolescents. *International Journal of Eating Disorders, 52*(12), 1445–1454. https://doi.org/10.1002/eat.23167; Maheux, A. J., Isom, K., & Marsh, H. W. (2020). Social media use and adolescent well-being: The role of quantity and quality of use. *Journal of Youth and Adolescence, 49*(8), 1717–1730. https://doi.org/10.1007/s10964-020-01270-8

18. Brundage, S. C., Ramos, M. A., & Shah, S. (2021). The intersection of youth mental health and academic achievement. *Health Affairs, 40*(6), 902–909. https://www.ncbi.nlm.nih.gov/pmc/articles/PMC8068628/; New Hampshire Department of Education. (n.d.). *Mental health and academic achievement.* https://www.education.nh.gov/sites/g/files/ehbemt326/files/inline-documents/mental_health_and_academic_achievement.pdf

19. Thompson, E. L., & Hasin, D. S. (2023). Long-term impact of adolescent mental health disorders on adult functioning: A review of recent findings. *Frontiers in Psychiatry, 14,* 10137824. https://www.ncbi.nlm.nih.gov/pmc/articles/PMC10137824/; Smith, J. P., & Smith, G. C. (2016). Long-term economic costs of psychological problems during childhood. *Social Science & Medicine, 154,* 166–173. https://www.sciencedirect.com/science/article/pii/S0277953616301137; https://

pmc.ncbi.nlm.nih.gov/articles/PMC10137824/   https://www.sciencedirect.com/science/article/pii/S0277953616301137?

20. Lund, C., Brooke-Sumner, C., Baingana, F., Baron, E. C., Breuer, E., Chandra, P., ... & Saxena, S. (2020). Social determinants of mental disorders and the Sustainable Development Goals: A systematic review of reviews. *The Lancet Psychiatry, 7*(4), 357–369. https://www.ncbi.nlm.nih.gov/pmc/articles/PMC7525587/; Haushofer, J., & Fehr, E. (2014). On the psychology of poverty. *Science, 344*(6186), 862–867. https://www.science.org/doi/10.1126/science.aay0214

11. The Opioid Crisis:

1. https://nida.nih.gov/research-topics/trends-statistics/overdose-death-rates

17. The System Is Blinking Red

1. National Institute on Drug Abuse. (2023). *Drug overdose deaths: Facts and figures.* https://nida.nih.gov/research-topics/trends-statistics/overdose-death-rates; Centers for Disease Control and Prevention (CDC). "U.S. Overdose Deaths Decrease in 2023, First Time Since 2018." Published May 14, 2024. Available at: https://www.cdc.gov/nchs/pressroom/nchs_press_releases/2024/20240515.htm; https://www.commonwealthfund.org/publications/2025/jan/us-overdose-deaths-remain-higher-other-countries

2. https://www.dea.gov/documents/2023-national-drug-threat-assessment

3. https://www.cdc.gov/nchs/products/databriefs/db509.htm; https://wonder.cdc.gov

4. Centers for Disease Control and Prevention. (2023). *Children's mental health data.* https://www.cdc.gov/childrensmentalhealth/data.html

5. National Institute on Drug Abuse. (2023). Drug topics and trends: Teen drug use statistics. https://nida.nih.gov/drug-topics/trends-statistics

6. National Institute on Drug Abuse. (2023). Monitoring the Future surveys: Trends in teen substance use. https://nida.nih.gov/drug-topics/trends-statistics/monitoring-future

7. U.S. Department of Education. (2021). Supporting child and student social, emotional, behavioral, and mental health. https://www.ed.gov/sites/ed/files/documents/students/supporting-child-student-social-emotional-behavioral-mental-health.pdf

8. U.S. Congress. (2022). Safer Communities Act of 2021, S.2938, 117th Congress. https://www.congress.gov/bill/117th-congress/senate-bill/2938

9. Education Week Research Center. (2019). Social-emotional learning: Perspectives from educators and district-level research. https://www.edweek.org/leadership/social-emotional-learning/2019/01

10. American Academy of Pediatrics, American Academy of Child and Adolescent Psychiatry, & Children's Hospital Association. (2021). AAP-AACAP-CHA declaration of a national emergency in child and adolescent mental health. https://publications.aap.org/news/2021/10/19/aap-aacap-cha-declaration-of-a-national-emergency-in-child-and-adolescent-mental-health

11. Association of School Business Officials International. (2019). School district spending priorities: Student wellness and prevention programs on the rise. https://asbointl.org

12. National Education Association. (2022). Survey: Alarming number of educators may leave profession soon. https://www.nea.org/research/publications-resources/survey-alarming-number-educators-may-leave-profession-soon

13. Collaborative for Academic, Social, and Emotional Learning (CASEL). (2020). What does the research say? https://casel.org/research

BIBLIOGRAPHY

Research For Programs

Clark, M. A., & Winters, K. C. (2002). Adolescent brain development and drugs. National Library of Medicine. https://www.ncbi.nlm.nih.gov/pmc/articles/PMC3399589/

Center on Addiction. (2019). Teen insights into drugs, alcohol, and nicotine: National survey on adolescent substance use._https://drugfree.org/wp-content/uploads/2019/06/CenteronAddiction_TeenInsightsintoDrugsAlcoholNicotine_June-2019.pdf

Center on Addiction. (2019). Teen insights into drugs, alcohol, and nicotine: National survey on adolescent substance use._https://drugfree.org/wp-content/uploads/2019/06/CenteronAddiction_TeenInsightsintoDrugsAlcoholNicotine_June-2019.pdf

Key Mental Health Strategies:

National Institute on Drug Abuse (NIDA). (n.d.). The connection between substance use disorders and mental illness. National Institutes of Health. https://nida.nih.gov/publications/research-reports/common-comorbidities-substance-use-disorders/part-1-connection-between-substance-use-disorders-mental-illness

National Institute on Drug Abuse (NIDA). (n.d.). The connection between substance use disorders and mental illness. National Institutes of Health. https://nida.nih.gov/publications/research-reports/common-comorbidities-substance-use-disorders/part-1-connection-between-substance-use-disorders-mental-illness

National Institute on Drug Abuse (NIDA). (n.d.). The connection between substance use disorders and mental illness. National Institutes of Health. https://nida.nih.gov/publications/research-reports/common-comorbidities-substance-use-disorders/part-1-connection-between-substance-use-disorders-mental-illness

Journaling

Research has demonstrated that keeping a journal leads to more optimism and gratitude, both of which can boost well-being. A 2018 study suggests that writing about positive experiences for just 15 minutes a day, three times a week, may help ease feelings of anxiety and stress and boost resilience (Psych Central, 2020).

Hubbs, D. L., & Brand, C. F. (2005). The paper mirror: Understanding reflective journaling. Journal of Experiential Education.

Baldwin, C. (1991). Life's companion: Journal writing as a spiritual quest. Bantam Books.

Moon, J. (1999). Learning journal: A handbook for academics, students, and professional development. Kogan Page.

Psych Central. (2020, February 11). The mental health benefits of journaling. Psych Central. https://psychcentral.com/lib/the-health-benefits-of-journaling

Exercise Interventions for Mental Health: A Quantitative and Qualitative Review

This article reviews the efficacy of exercise interventions for clinical populations diagnosed with depression, anxiety, and eating disorders, highlighting the substantial benefits observed in these groups. The authors conduct a meta-analysis of 11 treatment outcome studies involving individuals with depression, yielding a very large effect size for exercise over control conditions (g = 1.39, 95% CI: .89-1.88). The article discusses the potential mechanisms of action of exercise interventions, both biological and psychosocial, and encourages clinicians to consider integrating exercise into their practice (APA PsycNet, 2021).

Reference

APA PsycNet. (2021). *Exercise interventions for mental health: A quantitative and qualitative review.* https://psycnet.apa.org/record/2006-07167-009 (Hard copy available upon request)

Practicing Gratitude

Recent studies suggest that complementing psychological counseling with low-effort activities, like practicing gratitude, can significantly improve client outcomes. Research shows that people who consciously count their blessings tend to experience greater happiness and lower levels of depression. The following studies examine the benefits of gratitude practices in various settings, including classrooms and therapy:

Wilson, J. T. (2016). Brightening the mind: The impact of practicing gratitude on focus and resilience in learning. *Journal of the Scholarship of Teaching and Learning, 16*(4), 1-13.

Wilson, J., & Harris, P. (2015). Ripples of gratitude: The flow-on effects of practicing gratitude in the classroom environment. *International Christian Community of Teacher Educators Journal, 10*(1), 3.

Baumsteiger, R., Mangan, S., Bronk, K. C., & Bono, G. (2019). An integrative intervention for cultivating gratitude among adolescents and young adults. *The Journal of Positive Psychology, 14*(6), 807-819.

Psych Central. (2020, March 5). *Rewiring your brain for positivity with gratitude.* https://psychcentral.com/health/rewiring-your-brain-for-positivity-with-gratitude

Mindfulness-based Treatment of Addiction: Current State of the Field and Envisioning the Next Wave of Research

Mindfulness-based interventions (MBIs) have gained traction as treatments for addiction, with studies indicating that MBIs reduce substance misuse and cravings. This review examines how MBIs modulate cognitive, affective, and psychophysiological processes integral to self-regulation and reward processing. The authors suggest further research is needed to establish the efficacy of MBIs and explore their mechanisms in alleviating addiction (Biomed Central, 2018).

Reference

Biomed Central. (2018). Mindfulness-based treatment of addiction: Current state of the field and envisioning the next wave of research. *Addiction Science & Clinical Practice, 13*(1). https://ascpjournal.biomedcentral.com/articles/10.1186/s13722-018-0115-3

Mindfulness-Based Relapse Prevention to Reduce High-Risk Behaviors of People Addicted to Methamphetamine

This study investigates the effectiveness of Mindfulness-Based Relapse Prevention (MBRP) for reducing high-risk behaviors, such as aggression and craving, in people with methamphetamine dependence. The research demonstrates that MBRP significantly reduces these behaviors, with the experimental group showing substantial improvements compared to the control group (P < 0.01) (Brief Lands, 2021).

Reference

Brief Lands. (2021). Mindfulness-based relapse prevention to reduce high-risk behaviors of people addicted to methamphetamine. *International Journal of Health and Rehabilitation, 29*(1). https://brieflands.com/articles/ijhrba-92609.html

Anderson, S. L. (2018). Stress, sensitive periods, and substance abuse. Current Opinion in Behavioral Sciences, 19, 78–83. https://www.sciencedirect.com/science/article/pii/S2352289518300328

National Center for Biotechnology Information. (n.d.). Early detection of illicit drug use in teenagers. National Library of Medicine. https://www.ncbi.nlm.nih.gov/pmc/articles/PMC3257983/

Maurio, F. R. (2007). The strength within: 7 steps to overcoming life's obstacles with inspirational therapy. Estate Press.

National Center for Biotechnology Information. (n.d.). Adolescent gambling. National Library of Medicine. https://www.ncbi.nlm.nih.gov/pmc/articles/PMC2945873/

Substance Abuse and Mental Health Services Administration. (2016). Wellness practice, learning good habits, and overall well-being. https://store.samhsa.gov/sites/default/files/d7/priv/sma16-4958.pdf

Substance Abuse and Mental Health Services Administration. (n.d.). What is wellness? Retrieved from https://store.samhsa.gov/sites/default/files/d7/priv/sma16-4958.pdf

Sage Journals. (n.d.). Area-specific self-esteem, values, and adolescent substance use. Retrieved from https://journals.sagepub.com/doi/10.2190/DE.38.4.f

National Center for Biotechnology Information. (n.d.). Healthy decision making. Retrieved from https://www.ncbi.nlm.nih.gov/pmc/articles/PMC3399589/

Maurio, F. R. (2007). The strength within: 7 steps to overcoming life's obstacles with inspirational therapy. Estate Press.

Advokat, C. D., Comaty, J. E., & Julien, R. M. (2019). Julien's primer of drug action: A comprehensive guide to the actions, uses, and side effects of psychoactive drugs. Worth Publishers.

Nestler, E. J. (2001). Mechanisms of disease: Drug addiction. The New England Journal of Medicine, 345(20), 1364-1376. https://www.nejm.org/doi/full/10.1056/nejmra023160

Evidence-Based Strategies to Support Mental Well-Being

Active Listening

Research has shown that people often mimic others through words and gestures to create rapport and demonstrate similarity (Van Baaren et al., 2004). Positive social interactions, such as active listening, are linked to increased personal well-being and greater life satisfaction (M. Rost & Wilson, 2013).

- Van Baaren, R. B., Holland, R. W., Kawakami, K., & Van Knippenberg, A. (2004). Mimicry and prosocial behavior. Psychological Science, 15(1), 71-71.
- M. Rost, & J.J. Wilson. (2013). Active listening and well-being. Journal of Applied Social Psychology, 43(12), 2883-2891.
- Kabat-Zinn, J. (2003). Mindfulness-based interventions in context: Past, present, and future. Clinical Psychology: Science and Practice, 10, 144-156.

Breathing Exercises

Numerous studies indicate that breathing techniques can effectively combat anxiety and insomnia. These techniques impact both physiological and psychological factors by stimulating the parasympathetic nervous system and diverting attention from distressing thoughts (Tsai et al., 2015; Jerath et al., 2015).

- Tsai, H. J., et al. (2015). Efficacy of pacedamygdala-prefrontal cortex connectivity. NeuroImage, 134, 305-313.
- Zaccaro, A., et al. (2018). How breath control can change your life: A systematic review on psycho-physiological correlates of slow breathing. Frontiers in Human Neuroscience, 12, 353.

Conflict Resolution

- According to the Thomas-Kilmann Conflict Mode Instrument (TKI), used globally by human resource professionals, there are five primary styles of conflict management: collaborating, competing, avoiding, accommodating, and compromising.breathing for insomnia: Enhances vagal activity and improves sleep quality. Psychophysiology, 52(3), 388–396.
- Jerath, R., et al. (2015). Self-regulation of breathing as a primary treatment for anxiety. Applied Psychophysiology and Biofeedback, 40(2), 107–115.
- Doll, A. (2016). Mindful attention to breath regulates emotions via increased

Reference:

- Thomas-Kilmann Conflict Mode Instrument. The Kilmann-Saxton Culture-Gap® Survey and the Kilmann Organizational Conflict Instrument (KOCI).

Coping Strategies

Researchers have identified three main coping styles: problem-focused coping, emotion-focused coping, and avoidance coping. Problem-focused coping involves active efforts to resolve stressful situations (Austin, Shah, Muncer, 2006).
Reference:

- Austin, V., Shah, S. P. H., & Muncer, S. (2006). Teacher stress and coping strategies used to reduce stress. Journal of Educational Psychology, 98(2), 313-327.

Decision-Making Process

Decision-making involves identifying a decision, gathering information, and evaluating alternatives. A structured process helps individuals make deliberate, thoughtful choices by organizing relevant information (Lunenburg, 2010).

- Lunenburg, F. C. (2010). The decision-making process. National Forum of Educational Administration and Supervision Journal, 27(4), 1-8.
- Harrison, E. F. (1996). A process perspective on strategic decision making. Management Decision, 34(1), 46-53. https://doi.org/10.1108/00251749610106972

Effective Communication

Effective communication is linked to academic achievement, literacy development, and learning across subjects. It also plays a crucial role in social, emotional, and mental health (James et al., 2020).

- James, K., Munro, N., Togher, L., & Cordier, R. (2020). The spoken language and social communication characteristics of adolescents in behavioral schools: A controlled comparison study. Language, Speech, and Hearing Services in Schools, 51(1), 115-127. https://doi.org/10.1044/2019_LSHSS-18-0090
- Roulstone, S., et al. (2011). Investigating the role of language in children's early educational outcomes. Bristol University Press.

Emotion Labeling

Emotion labeling, or affect labeling, refers to naming emotions with greater specificity, helping to decrease the amygdala's activation and reduce stress reactions (Burklund et al., 2014).

- Burklund, L. J., Creswell, J. D., Irwin, M. R., & Lieberman, M. D. (2014). The common and distinct neural bases of affect labeling and reappraisal in healthy adults. Frontiers in Psychology, 5, 221. https://doi.org/10.3389/fpsyg.2014.00221

- Lieberman, M. D., Inagaki, T. K., Tabibnia, G., & Crockett, M. J. (2011). Subjective responses to emotional stimuli during labeling, reappraisal, and distraction. Emotion, 11(3), 468-480. https://doi.org/10.1037/a0023503

Emotions Check-in

Emotions check-ins help learners build self-awareness and provide a proactive tool for problem-solving. These practices bring calm and mindfulness to the day (Wang, 2013).

Reference:

- Wang, S. S. (2013). "I share, therefore I am": Personality traits, life satisfaction, and Facebook check-ins. Cyberpsychology, Behavior, and Social Networking, 16(12), 870-877. https://doi.org/10.1089/cyber.2013.0224

Finding Your Individuality

Self-identity is flexible and can adapt to different roles and situations (Aronson, 1969).

- Dweck, C. S. (2007). Mindset: The new psychology of success. Random House.
- Yeager, D. S., & Dweck, C. S. (2020). What can be learned from growth mindset controversies? American Psychologist, 75(9), 1269–1284. https://doi.org/10.1037/amp0000794

I Can Statements

'I Can' statements help students understand the lesson's goals, why they are important, and how to demonstrate learning. These statements track learning progress (Brookhart & Moss, 2014).

- Brookhart, S., & Moss, C. (2014). Learning targets on parade. Educational Leadership, 72(1), 28-33.
- Marzano, R. (2010). When students track their progress. Educational Leadership, 67(4), 86-87.

Identifying Happy Places

Visualization is an effective technique for understanding and measuring data, which has been shown to impact well-being through urban transformations (Cassarino et al., 2021).

Reference:

- Cassarino, M., Shahab, S., & Biscaya, S. (2021). Envisioning happy places for all: A systematic review of the impact of transformations in the urban environment on the well-being of vulnerable groups. Sustainability, 13(14), 8086. https://doi.org/10.3390/su13148086

Journaling

Research suggests that journaling can enhance optimism and gratitude, which contribute to overall well-being. Writing about positive experiences can alleviate anxiety and stress (Hubbs & Brand, 2005).

- Hubbs, D. L., & Brand, C. F. (2005). The paper mirror: Understanding reflective journaling. Journal of Experiential Education, 28(2), 128-138.
- Baldwin, C. (1991). Life's companion: Journal writing as a spiritual quest. Bantam Books.

Metacognition

Studies show that metacognition, or self-regulation of cognitive processes, is associated with successful learning outcomes (Dunlosky & Metcalfe, 2008).

- Dunlosky, J., & Metcalfe, J. (2008). Metacognition. Sage Publications.
- Blakey, E., & Spence, S. (1990). Developing metacognition. ERIC Clearinghouse on Information and Technology.

Mindfulness

Mindfulness has a wide range of psychological benefits, including reducing anxiety and depression and improving emotional regulation (Shapiro et al., 2006; Hofmann & Gómez, 2017).

- Shapiro, S. L., Carlson, L. E., Astin, J. A., & Freedman, B. (2006). Mechanisms of mindfulness. Journal of Clinical Psychology, 62(3), 373-386. https://doi.org/10.1002/jclp.20237
- Hofmann, S. G., & Gómez, A. F. (2017). Mindfulness-based interventions for anxiety and depression: A review of meta-analytic findings. Journal of Clinical Psychology, 73(7), 1006-1022. https://doi.org/10.1002/jclp.22403

Character Building Themes and Social Emotional Learning

CASEL. (n.d.). What is SEL? Collaborative for Academic, Social, and Emotional Learning. Retrieved from https://www.casel.org/what-is-SEL

Centers for Disease Control and Prevention. (n.d.). Adolescent and school health: Healthy youth development. Retrieved from https://www.cdc.gov/healthyyouth

New York State Education Department. (n.d.). New York State social emotional learning benchmarks. Retrieved from https://www.p12.nysed.gov/sss/documents/NYSSEL-Benchmarks.pdf

New York State Education Department. (n.d.). New York State social emotional learning benchmarks webpage. Retrieved from https://www.p12.nysed.gov/sss/selbenchmarks.html

CASEL. (n.d.). Fundamentals of SEL: What does the research say? Collaborative for

Academic, Social, and Emotional Learning. Retrieved from https://casel.org/funda-mentals-of-sel/what-does-the-research-say/

https://casel.org/fundamentals-of-sel/what-is-the-casel-framework/

Connecting Stakeholders

CASEL. (n.d.). What is SEL? Collaborative for Academic, Social, and Emotional Learning. Retrieved from https://www.casel.org/what-is-SEL

The research suggests that connecting children with key stakeholders, such as family, school, and their broader social ecosystem, can significantly reduce the risk of drug use and improve mental health during pivotal years. This approach is rooted in CASEL's Social and Emotional Learning (SEL) framework, which emphasizes the development of healthy identities, emotional management, and the ability to make responsible decisions (CASEL, n.d.).

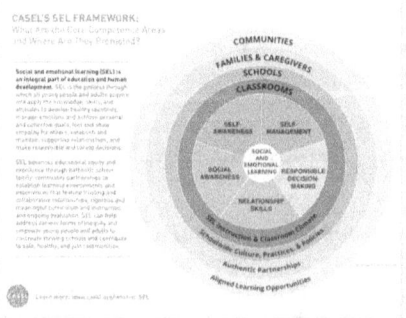

Recurring Individualized Communicative Addiction Prevention Program (RICAPP)

National Center for Biotechnology Information. (2012). Early detection of illicit drug use in teenagers. **Retrieved from https://www.ncbi.nlm.nih.gov/pmc/articles/PMC3257983/**

V. Early Identification and Intervention Action Teams For Children At Risk

American Medical Association. (2016). Promoting access to school-based services for children's mental health. Journal of Ethics. Retrieved from https://journalofethics.ama-assn.org/article/promoting-access-school-based-services-childrens-mental-health/2016-12

American Medical Association. (2016). Addressing the problem of youth mental health services through an effective school model. Journal of Ethics. Retrieved from https://journalofethics.ama-assn.org/article/promoting-access-school-based-services-childrens-mental-health/2016-12

Littleton Public Schools. (2015). Improving mental health in schools: Intervention, MTSS, and other supports. Retrieved from https://littletonpublicschools.net/sites/default/files/MENTAL%20HEALTH%20-%20Improving%20MH%20in%20Schools%202015.pdf

ABOUT THE AUTHOR

Paul Vecchione is the Founder and CEO of Long Island PREP, an organization dedicated to substance abuse prevention, mental health awareness, and crisis intervention in schools. With over 20 years of experience as an educator, Paul has worked extensively with students, families, and school districts to develop innovative programs that address the growing challenges of addiction and mental health in young people.

A passionate advocate for education and youth empowerment, Paul brings a deeply personal touch to his life's work. Born and raised in Long Island, New York, he grew up in a tight-knit family in a wonderful suburban community, surrounded by the strong foundational pillars of family and education. Now raising three young boys in a neighboring community with his wife, Melanie, Paul draws on his own experiences to bring about meaningful change and create a brighter future for his children, his students, and people everywhere.

Visit Paul Vecchione https://www.longislandprep.org/

Connect with Paul on Facebook: https://www.facebook.com/longislandprep

OTHER BOOKS BY PAUL VECCHIONE

In addition to this work, Paul has written a children's book, *Blueberries and Touchdowns. Joshua's Best Day With Mom and Dad.*

For more information on all his titles, please visit his Amazon Author Page.

LEAVE ME A REVIEW

If you enjoyed this book or found it useful, please take a moment to leave a review on Amazon or Goodreads. I'm always interested in learning what you like, think, and want. I read all the reviews personally.

Thank you for your support!

REFLECTIONS (NOTES)